Es: **al**

Health Law

ONE WEEK LOAN

Essential Mental Health Law

a guide to
the revised Mental Health Act
and
the Mental Capacity Act 2005

Anthony Maden
and
Tim Spencer-Lane

Hammersmith Press
London, UK

First published in 2010 by Hammersmith Press Limited
14 Greville Street, London EC1N 8SB, UK
www.hammersmithpress.co.uk

British Library Cataloguing in Publication Data: A CIP record of this book is
available from the British Library.

ISBN 978-1-905140-29-9

Commissioning editor: Georgina Bentliff
Designed and typeset by: Julie Bennett
Proof reading by: Brackley Proof Reading Services
Index by: Claudia Kinmonth
Production by: Helen Whitehorn, Pathmedia
Printed and bound by: TJ International
Cover image: © Corbis

Contents

About the authors

Professor Anthony Maden

Professor Anthony Maden FRCPsych is Professor of Forensic Psychiatry, Division of Neurosciences and Mental Health, Imperial College, London University, and Clinical Director of the Dangerous and Severe Personality Disorder Service with West London Mental Health Trust.

Tim Spencer-Lane

Tim Spencer-Lane, a lawyer, works at the Law Commission where he is responsible for the review of adult social care law. He worked previously as the Policy Advisor on mental health and disability law for the Law Society and was co-Chair of the Mental Health Alliance Policy Group. He is also an Associate Lecturer with the Open University and is the Academic Chair for the social work law course.

Chapter 9 on Children and Young People was reviewed by **Elizabeth Fellow-Smith** Medical Director, West London Mental Health NHS Trust.

Introduction

Mental health legislation is one of the most contentious areas of law because it provides a framework under which individuals can be detained and treated without their consent. Much of the debate arises out of a clash between social goals: the need to provide adequate mental health care and treatment to those suffering from a mental disorder, and, on the other hand, the need to protect individuals from unwarranted restraint on personal liberty. The use of mental health law therefore raises fundamental questions about personal autonomy and liberty, the role of the state, the clinical judgement of medical practitioners and other professionals and complex questions of medical science and ethics.

The principal statutes in England and Wales governing this area of law are the Mental Health Act 1983 and the Mental Capacity Act 2005. Both of these Acts enable care and treatment to be provided to individuals without their consent, albeit in different ways and often different circumstances. Many specialist mental health practitioners, including psychiatrists, nurses and social workers, will have a detailed understanding of this legislation once fully trained. Furthermore, a separate branch of the law has now grown up around mental health law, with certain lawyers specialising in this area.

However, mental health law is also of relevance to so-called non-specialist clinicians and practitioners. These include general practitioners, general nurses, social care professionals, private client lawyers, occupational therapists, the emergency services, probation workers, student nurses and social workers. All of these groups may be required to carry out certain tasks under this legislation, such as an assessment of mental capacity or an assessment under the Mental Health Act, or they may be working with people who are, or have been, subject to the powers of the Mental Health Act.

This book is intended to be both an introduction to the principles of mental health legislation for future specialists still in training, and a practical guide for the non-specialists. By focusing on what current legislation means in practice, it may also provide a useful reference or summary for specialist mental health practitioners.

The last 15 years have witnessed a tumultuous period in mental health law reform. The Mental Capacity Act is the culmination of a long consultation process dating back to a Law Commission review launched in 1989. Plans to overhaul the Mental Health Act were announced by the then government in 1998 and, following two aborted draft Bills, eventually led to the Mental Health Act 2007 which amended substantially the 1983 Act. Together these reforms have caused great controversy, but now that they are in place there is a need to understand what they mean for the individual practitioner when making decisions about the care and treatment of vulnerable individuals.

Chapter 1

Mental Disorder

The revised Mental Health Act 1983 adopts a broad definition of mental disorder as 'any disorder or disability of the mind'. Under the original 1983 Act there were four categories of mental disorder. Dropping these is arguably one of the most important of all the 2007 revisions, although the existence of a mental disorder is never sufficient grounds for the use of compulsion under the Act. The change is intended to reinforce one of the Guiding Principles of the new Act, which deals with the purpose of the legislation:

> *Decisions under the Act must be taken with a view to minimising the undesirable effects of mental disorder, by maximising the safety and wellbeing (mental and physical) of patients, promoting their recovery and protecting other people from harm.*[1]

The Purpose Principle is (literally) the first principle behind the new legislation. A broad definition of mental disorder is intended to reduce unnecessary constraints on professionals and to focus attention on the primary purpose of minimising the undesirable effects of mental disorder. There is also an implicit appeal to commonsense, or to lay rather than professional values: esoteric debate about the diagnosis of mental disorder should not be allowed to interfere with the more important process of risk management.

---

[1] Department of Health, *Code of Practice: Mental Health Act 1983* (2008) para: 1.2.

Which mental disorders are included?

Given the broad definition above, 'which mental disorders are included?' is almost a meaningless question. Human rights law requires that, for detention on the grounds of mental illness to be lawful, the presence or absence of mental illness must be established by objective medical exper- tise. The test will be a reasonable body of medical opinion and the point of reference, one or other of the major diagnostic manuals – that is, *The International Classification of Mental and Behavioural Disorders (ICD)*[2] or *The Diagnostic and Statistical Manual (DSM)*.[3]

Except for those manuals, any list is likely to be incomplete. *The Code of Practice* emphasises the inclusiveness of the definition by listing examples of 'clinically recognised conditions which could fall within the Act's definition of mental disorder'.

They are, in the no particular order used in the *Code*, as follows:

- Affective disorders, such as depression and bipolar disorder;

- Schizophrenia and delusional disorders;

- Neurotic, stress-related and somatoform disorders including anxiety and phobic disorders;

- Obsessive compulsive disorders;

- Post-traumatic stress disorder;

- Hypochondriacal disorders;

- Organic mental disorders such as dementia and delirium (however caused);

- Personality and behavioural changes caused by brain injury or damage (however acquired);

- Personality disorders;

- Mental and behavioural disorders caused by psychoactive substance use;

---

[2] World Health Organization (WHO). (1993). *The ICD-10 classification of mental and behavioural disorders: Diagnostic criteria for research*. Geneva, Switzerland: WHO.
[3] American Psychiatric Association (APA). (1994). *Diagnostic and statistical manual of mental disorders* (4th ed.). Washington, DC: APA.

- Eating disorders;

- Non-organic sleep disorders;

- Non-organic sexual disorders;

- Learning disabilities subject to certain qualifications;

- Autistic spectrum disorders (including Asperger's syndrome);

- Behavioural and emotional disorders of children and adolescents.

The message is clear. Virtually nothing is ruled out. So long as there is a disorder or disability of mind, the use of the Act should not be subject to the vagaries, whims or fashions of psychiatric diagnosis.

Reasons for the change

In physical medicine the pathologist is the ultimate arbiter, but with a few exceptions, such as Alzheimer's disease, psychiatric diagnosis has less solid foundations. Most conditions have the status of syndromes, or clusters of symptoms, rather than diseases with an established pathological basis.

As a consequence, psychiatric diagnosis is in a constant state of flux. New editions of the major classification systems are published regularly. Diagnoses disappear and new ones are created, whilst the enduring conditions are re-ordered and renamed.

Far from being an indictment of psychiatry, that state of change is the inevitable result of its scientific basis. Science begins with classification and as new knowledge emerges it is inevitable that earlier classifications are abandoned. Unfortunately, good science may not be the best foundation for good law. It is not practical to revise legislation to suit every new edition of *The Diagnostic and Statistical Manual* – and if it were practical, why choose that system rather than *The International Classification of Mental and Behavioural Disorders*?

Rather than struggling to keep up with scientific progress, it was considered that a better solution is to couch the law in more general terms. If mental disorders are broadly defined then esoteric diagnostic debates can be sidestepped. Tribunals are able to concentrate on the more important questions surrounding deprivation of liberty, which has always been much more than a medical or scientific question.

The 2007 revision is one of degree. The 1983 Act, prior to the 2007 revisions, accepted the principle of trusting diagnosis to the professionals by, for example, leaving mental illness undefined. However, it departed from that approach and was more prescriptive in the case of other disorders, namely psychopathic disorder and mental impairment. The Government argued that the law was most controversial, if not unworkable, when it ventured into areas that were more appropriate for scientific debate. The advent of the revised Act consigns this controversy to history, but it is worth brief consideration because it sheds light on the principles underlying the new legislation.

Psychopathic disorder in the 1983 Act

The category of psychopathic disorder was felt to be controversial, first because of circularity in the definition. It was defined in terms of being abnormally aggressive or showing seriously irresponsible conduct, whilst at the same time psychopathic disorder was seen as the cause of that conduct. This, it was argued, compounded diagnosis and risk.

Developments in the diagnosis of personality disorder

The underlying problem was an attempt to simplify issues that are inherently complicated. Methods of diagnosing personality disorder have changed greatly over the 25 years since the 1983 Act. The training of psychiatrists in the task has improved from a baseline that was close to zero. It is now acknowledged that there is a balance to be struck between self-report and reliance on historical records, whilst debate continues about where the balance lies. A brief statutory definition could never do justice to these developments.

One of the major advances over the last 25 years was the development of an operational measure of psychopathy,[4] which allowed professionals to describe the degree of the condition in a common language for the first time.

---

[4] Hare RD (1991) *The Psychopathy Checklist Revised*. Toronto: Multi-Health Systems.

Diagnosis versus risk assessment

The development of new measures of personality disorder and psychopathy stimulated research into the associated risks to self and others, including the risks of violence and antisocial behaviour. At the same time, there was a massive growth in research on the risks associated with other mental disorders. One of the robust findings to emerge from this work is that the association between individual diagnosis and risk can never be assumed.

The circular definition of psychopathy in the 1983 Act confused diagnosis and risk. The revised Act treats them as separate questions and gives professionals two separate but related duties. The first is to make a diagnosis – that is, to establish the presence of a mental disorder. The second is to make an assessment of the associated risks.

Personality disorder and treatability

The second cause of controversy surrounding the legal category of psychopathic disorder was the requirement that detention was permissible only if treatment would alleviate or prevent deterioration in the condition. It was argued that one of the problems with the so-called treatability test is that it is rarely possible to guarantee any medical treatment will be effective in an individual patient. The most that can be said is the treatment has been shown to be more effective than placebo in similar patients. The Government claimed that the revised Act's reliance on availability of appropriate treatment and the requirement that the purpose of any medical treatment must be to alleviate or prevent a worsening of the disorder or one of its symptoms or manifestations, is more consistent with the underlying science.

It was also suggested that the law should refer back to a lay or commonsense view of medical services and that most people struggle to understand why a person who presents a high risk to others and is not responsive to treatment should be discharged from detention in hospital. Analogies were made with other fields of medicine which, on the rare occasions they deal in third-party risk, place lack of response to treatment firmly on the other side of the scale. Legal powers exist for restricting the liberty of patients who are likely to spread an infectious disease and it was argued that those powers are more likely to be used when the condition is resistant to treatment or when patients are uncooperative.

5

Further it was suggested that the meaning of the treatability test has become meaningless. Tribunals were often reluctant to release high-risk patients on the grounds of lack of response to treatment. Case law shows a widening of the concept of treatment to include basic nursing care in a secure environment. The new test of availability of appropriate treatment and the purpose of medical treatment, it was argued, would encourage an emphasis on the provision of proper treatment programmes.

It was, in addition, claimed that the new wording would also address the difficulty of distinguishing between patients who cannot be helped and those who refuse to engage in treatment. Interventions for personality disorder are often psychological and depend on the patient's willingness to engage. The old Act, it was claimed, contained a potential disincentive to treatment because refusal to engage might be presented as evidence of being untreatable and the new wording would reduce that problem.

Personality disorder and social exclusion

The preceding discussion was concerned mainly with Tribunals and patients in high security hospitals. That is no accident. Detention in hospital is rarely an appropriate treatment for patients with personality disorder and is generally considered only for a minority of patients presenting a high risk when alternative ways of managing risk have been exhausted.

Yet the impact of these extreme cases has been widespread. Esoteric arguments over treatability in high-risk patients may have encouraged a general pessimism and reluctance to provide services to patients with personality disorder in other settings. The diagnosis may mean that patients seeking help are turned away from services without proper assessment. When there are concerns about self-harm or violence, assessment of risk may proceed no further than the diagnosis of personality disorder, at which point it is abandoned because the condition is 'untreatable'.

At the dramatic end of the spectrum some of these excluded patients go on to commit serious offences. In some, the diagnosis is shown to be wrong and to have resulted in denial of treatment for schizophrenia or other serious mental illness. At a more mundane level, discrimination based on diagnosis alone is at variance with a wider policy of social inclusion, as argued in the Department of Health's policy initiative, *Personality* *Disorder: no longer a diagnosis of exclusion*. It is claimed that the desire to

6

counter social exclusion is one of the principles underpinning the new Act.

Critics have argued the legal changes amount to pressure to detain large numbers of patients with a personality disorder. The *Code of Practice*, however, sets out that:

> *No assumptions should be made about the suitability of using the Act – or indeed providing services without using the Act – in respect of personality disorders or the people who have them. The factors which should inform decisions are the needs of the individual patient, the risks posed by their disorder and what can be done to address those needs and risks, in both the short and longer term.*[5]

It goes on to explain that patients must be properly assessed in a manner appropriate to the circumstances and that it is not acceptable to omit assessment just because the diagnosis is thought to be personality disorder.

Personality disorder in the revised Act

No distinction is made between personality disorder and other forms of mental disorder. When considering use of the Act, the same criteria are to be used as are applied to any other mental disorder, including mental illnesses.

Exclusions in the revised Act

Exclusions provide that a person cannot be dealt with as mentally disordered solely on the basis of specific conditions or diagnoses. The only specific exclusion in the revised 1983 Act is dependence on alcohol or drugs. Special conditions are attached to the circumstances under which a diagnosis of learning disability alone can be the basis for compulsory treatment.

Dependence on alcohol or drugs

For the purposes of the definition of mental disorder in the Act, dependence on alcohol or drugs is not considered to be a disorder or disability of

---

[5] Department of Health, *Code of Practice: Mental Health Act 1983* (2008) para: 3.19.

the mind (Section 1(3)). Similar considerations apply to misuse of alcohol or drugs that falls short of dependence.

No distinctions are made between different drugs and the term for these purposes includes volatile solvents. The exclusion will apply to any new drugs of misuse that may emerge in the future. No person may be subject to the use of compulsory powers under the Act for substance misuse or dependence alone.

It would be wrong to interpret the unequivocal terms of this exclusion as allowing mental health professionals to disregard drug and alcohol problems when using the new Act. On the contrary, such problems are likely to feature in many if not most cases of patients subject to compulsion because alcohol and drugs are so commonly associated with problems of diagnosis, risk assessment and rehabilitation.

Associations with other mental disorders

Dependence on alcohol or drugs is frequently associated with other mental disorders and the Act applies to these associated disorders or disabilities of mind. For these purposes, it does not matter if the mental disorder caused the dependence, if the dependence caused the mental disorder, or if the association is coincidental. In practice, it is often impossible to tease out the causal links.

Disorders likely to be encountered in this context include withdrawal states with associated delirium or psychotic disorder, and organic mental disorders associated with prolonged abuse of drugs or alcohol. Depression is common in those who misuse alcohol or drugs.

Drug-induced psychosis may present problems, but the situation is unambiguous; in terms of the Act, it is a mental disorder to be treated in the same way as any other mental disorder. It follows that the distinction between drug-induced psychosis and a psychosis accompanied by drug use is of no real importance for the purposes of assessment under the Act. Both are mental disorders and the other criteria for detention are to be applied in exactly the same way.

Drugs, alcohol and risk

Whilst the causal links between substance misuse and mental disorder may be complicated, the association between substances and risk is a simple one: substance misuse in association with mental disorder increases any present risks to self and others. This topic is considered in more detail in the following chapter. It is mentioned here as a reminder that drug and alcohol use must be considered in all assessments.

Compulsory treatment of alcohol or drug misuse

The *Code of Practice* states:

> *Medical treatment for mental disorder under the Act (including treatment with consent) can include measures to address alcohol or drug dependence if that is an appropriate part of treating the mental disorder which is the primary focus of the treatment.*[6]

If a patient is subject to compulsion under the Act, for example, because of schizophrenia or personality disorder, treatment for alcohol or drug misuse/dependence may be a central part of the treatment programme. In some cases, it may determine the speed of progress in recovery.

Learning disabilities

For the purposes of the Act, a learning disability is defined as 'a state of arrested or incomplete development of the mind which includes significant impairment of intelligence and social functioning'.[7]

Learning disabilities are mental disorders in terms of the Act, but additional conditions have been placed on the use of some compulsory powers. As the *Code of Practice* points out, relatively few people with learning disabilities are detained under the Act. It is rare for them to be detained solely because of the learning disability rather than other disorders that accompany it.

The 'learning disability qualification' states that if a person suffers from learning disabilities then they cannot be considered on the basis of this disability to be mentally disordered unless the condition is accompanied by abnormally aggressive or seriously irresponsible conduct in order for the following powers to be used:

---

[6] Department of Health, *Code of Practice: Mental Health Act 1983* (2008) para: 3.12.
[7] Mental Health Act 1983 Section 1.4.

- Detention in hospital for treatment;
- Guardianship;
- Supervised Community Treatment (SCT);
- Criminal justice orders under Part 3 of the Act.

The learning disability qualification does not apply to other sections of the Act. For example, detention for assessment under Section 2 of the Act is determined by the same criteria as apply to other forms of mental disorder.

The learning disability qualification does not apply to autistic spectrum disorders (including Asperger's syndrome), which are treated in the same way as all other mental disorders. Autistic spectrum disorders are frequently associated with learning difficulties but in these cases the learning disability qualification does not apply.

The same principle applies to the presence of any co-morbid mental disorder with learning disability; the other mental disorder 'trumps' the learning disability.

The learning disability qualification continues to apply when a learning disability is complicated by alcohol or drug dependence because these latter conditions do not count as mental disorders in terms of the Act.

The process of diagnosing mental disorder

Neither the Act nor the *Code of Practice* has much to say on the subject of how to arrive at a diagnosis of mental disorder. That reticence is consistent with the general principle of leaving technical matters to the professionals. The following guidance is to an extent speculative but based on the principles underlying the Act and other related legislation.

The diagnosis is likely to be tested against the standard of a reasonable body of medical opinion and it should be consistent with one of the standard classification systems. It would be reasonable for a Tribunal to ask for the diagnosis to be presented as one of the categories listed in those systems and it would be a cause for concern if that were not possible.

The balance between mental state and history

Errors in mental health assessments often result from excessive reliance on a single mental state examination. In some cases, particularly in emergencies, that may be all that is available, but reasonable efforts should be made to obtain additional information from records or from informants. The latter will often be relations or carers and, in addition to the statutory requirements for their involvement, they are often a source of vital clinical information.

Both history and mental state are important in diagnosis. Usually they point in the same direction. When they conflict, steps should be taken to resolve that conflict by obtaining further information, whether relating to the history, further interviews or observation. When the conflict cannot be resolved, there are good reasons to give greater weight to the history. Some surgeons teach that 90% of diagnostic information comes from the history and only 10% from examination. Even if the imbalance is less in mental health, the same principle applies.

Conflict may also arise between the patient and a carer, with the former insisting nothing is wrong and the latter convinced of the presence of a serious mental disorder. The same principles apply to resolution as when the conflict is between mental state and history. The Act encourages the involvement of carers, and their views should be given full and appropriate consideration. If the decision reached is not that desired by the carer, a full explanation should be given and documented in the medical notes.

Use of standardised diagnostic instruments

Many people are drawn to standardised diagnostic instruments because of the apparent precision they bring to a murky area. Unfortunately, the process of psychiatric diagnosis is inherently flawed, so with a few exceptions the precision is spurious and use of these instruments may be misleading and harmful.

Most standardised diagnostic instruments depend on self-report of symptoms. Almost all were developed for research purposes. They are based on three related assumptions. First, the interaction is between researcher and subject with no third party involved; second, symptoms are reported honestly; and third, there is no external pressure to reach a particular conclusion because nothing of any consequence depends on what is found.

None of these assumptions applies to assessments under the Act. Third parties may be involved as carers or informants. In assessments of violence risk, the safety of others is a major concern. There are powerful pressures acting against honest reporting of symptoms because the outcome of the assessment may have profound consequences for the individual. Even in individuals who are attempting to be honest, their ability to report on their own symptoms may be impaired by a lack of insight. Lack of insight is, of course, more likely in the acute illnesses or crisis situations often encountered in assessments under the Act.

It is for these reasons that the clinical history and the accounts of informants are of such importance. Assessment is essentially a clinical process and no standardised diagnostic instrument can substitute for that process.

There are important exceptions to this general principle. Standardised diagnostic assessments should not be used in isolation, but they are likely to be of value in enhancing clinical assessment in the following conditions:

- Learning disability;
- Autistic spectrum disorders;
- Personality disorders.

Learning disability

Learning disability is straightforward because a measure of intelligence is essential. There is general agreement that learning disability begins at IQ 69 or below, which indicates more than two standard deviations from the population mean.

Even in learning disability, the standardised measure is not the final arbiter. Except at very low levels, an IQ score does not necessarily indicate learning disability, which depends on functional impairments. Again the diagnostic process is clinical, but it should always be supplemented by a standardised measure of intelligence.

Autistic spectrum disorders

The diagnosis of autistic spectrum disorder requires a developmental history from a third party. A clinical assessment should ideally be supplemented by a structured checklist. Whilst all mental health professionals should have an awareness of these conditions, a definitive diagnosis should ideally be carried out by a specialist in the field, so further details are beyond the scope of this text.

Despite these comments, the non-specialist should not necessarily be deterred from making an assessment. In most cases, the original diagnosis will be clear from medical records that include the specialist assessment. In such a case, the diagnosis is not a major issue and the task of the professional is one of risk assessment following the same principles that apply to other mental disorders (see Chapter 2).

Personality disorders

It is here that standardised or structured assessments will be of greatest importance. The *Code of Practice* states:

> *Professionals will need to ensure that any treatment and aftercare plans are shaped by appropriate clinical assessments conducted by suitably trained practitioners.*[8]

The same principle applies to diagnosis. Many mental health professionals have not had extensive training or experience in the diagnosis of personality disorder. Even if they have extensive training and experience, the structured assessment helps with organisation of complex clinical data.

The diagnosis of personality disorder presents specific challenges:

- Diagnosis depends less on mental state than on history;
- Self-report may be particularly unreliable; information from records and third parties is of even greater importance than in other assessments;
- Other disorders may resemble personality disorder and it is vital not to overlook psychosis or depression;

---

[8] Department of Health, *Code of Practice: Mental Health Act 1983* (2008) para: 35.6.

- It is necessary to distinguish personality disorder from other causes of antisocial behaviour;

- Antisocial personality disorder is common in prison and forensic settings and professionals need to be able reliably to distinguish degrees of severity.

In crisis or high-risk situations, extensive assessment will not be possible. The *Code of Practice* states that in such situations 'the immediate risk to the health or safety of the patient or to other people is the first priority'[9] so a lack of information should not prevent necessary action. However, a fuller assessment should be completed as soon as possible thereafter.

Although a full account is beyond the scope of this text, the most useful instruments are likely to be:

- International Personality Disorder Examination[10] (IPDE)

- Personality Assessment Schedule[11] (PAS)

- Psychopathy Checklist – Screening Version[12] (PCL-SV)

Brief notes on their use follow.

The International Personality Disorder Examination (IPDE)

- The main value of the IPDE is as a well-established tool for making ICD and DSM diagnoses for research;

- Widely regarded as the gold standard for diagnosis;

- Relies on self-report so of doubtful value in forensic practice or where insight is impaired;

- Much too long for general use;

- Requires training and time so will be restricted to specialist services.

---

[9] Department of Health, *Code of Practice: Mental Health Act 1983* (2008) para: 35.7.

[10] Loranger, AW (1999). *IPDE: International Personality Disorder Examination: DSM-IV and ICD-10 Interviews*. Odessa, FL: Psychological Assessment Resources, Inc.

[11] Tyrer P & Alexander J (1988) Personality Assessment Schedule.In: Tyrer P (Ed) *Personality Disorders*. London: Wright.

[12] Hart S, Cox D & Hare R (1995) *The Hare Psychopathy Checklist -: Screening Version*. Toronto: Multi-Health Systems.

The Personality Assessment Schedule (PAS)

- Training demands are minimal;

- Brief and practical for non-specialists;

- Not reliant on self-report.

The Psychopathy Checklist – Screening Version (PCL-SV)

- A quantitative measure of psychopathy or antisocial personality disorder;

- Not reliant on self-report;

- Widely used;

- Training essential;

- Links readily to risk assessment of violence;

- The full Psychopathy Checklist - Revised (PCL-R) is used by specialist services, mainly in forensic settings.

Structured assessments are also helpful in the assessment of treatment needs and risks. These topics are covered in Chapter 2.

Chapter 2

Compulsory Admission to Hospital and Renewal

Part 2 of the Act allows for the detention in hospital of patients who have not been convicted of a crime. This form of detention is known as 'civil commitment' in the USA. In the UK it is sometimes known as 'civil' detention to distinguish such patients from mentally disordered offenders detained under Part 3 of the Act (see Chapter 10).

Whilst separate Parts of the Act deal with civil patients and mentally disordered offenders, the underlying principles are similar. It is axiomatic that patients subject to the Act all suffer from severe forms of mental disorder and there may be no clinical distinction between civil patients and mentally disordered offenders.

At one extreme, some patients commit crimes that inevitably lead to conviction; at the other, some patients never break the law despite suffering from the most severe forms of mental disorder. In the middle ground are many cases in which mental disorder leads to law-breaking but with no inevitable progression to conviction. The outcome may be a matter of chance depending on whether bystanders call the doctor or the police. It may also be the result of a reasoned decision to pursue one or other course of action in line with a policy of diversion from the criminal justice system.

Full consideration of the debate on diversion from the criminal justice system is beyond the scope of this text but three points should be noted:

- Diversion involves legal and moral considerations so it is not solely a medical matter;

- The UK Government has a policy of diverting mentally disordered offenders away from the criminal justice system whenever possible;

- In marginal cases, civil detention is to be preferred, but the choice of a civil route does not imply any less need for appropriate risk management.

Detention in hospital under Part 2 of the Act

The Act allows detention for assessment under Section 2 or for treatment under Section 3.

Criteria for detention for assessment under Section 2

Both the following must apply:

- Suffering from a mental disorder of a nature or degree which warrants detention in hospital for assessment (or for assessment followed by treatment) for at least a limited period; and

- The person ought to be so detained in the interests of their own health or safety or with a view to the protection of others.

Criteria for detention for treatment under Section 3

All three of the following must apply:

- Suffering from a mental disorder of a nature or degree which makes it appropriate for the patient to receive medical treatment in hospital; and

- It is necessary for the health or safety of the person or for the protection of other persons that he/she should receive such treatment and it cannot be provided unless the patient is detained under this Section; and

- Appropriate medical treatment is available.

Notes on the criteria for detention

'mental disorder'
See Chapter 1.

'nature or degree'
Both nature and degree must be considered. 'Nature' refers to the diagnosis and clinical features of the patient's mental disorder. It depends largely on history, even when the history is short as in a first episode of mental disorder. Important features may include:

- Risky behaviours, preoccupations or threats;

- Deliberate self-harm or suicidal thoughts;

- Violence;

- Insight;

- Attitude towards treatment;

- Compliance;

- Response to treatment;

- Chronicity;

- Prognosis.

'Degree' refers to the current symptoms and manifestations of the patient's disorder. Many of the relevant features are the same as those listed above for nature but the emphasis is on the here and now rather than on history.

The word 'or' deserves as much emphasis as the other two terms. It means what it says. Its significance is greatest in cases where the nature of the disorder is severe, as indicated by a history of, for example, life-threatening self-harm or violence. In a chronic or recurrent disorder there is no necessity to await a particular degree of deterioration before using the Act. In fact, given historical evidence of the nature of the disorder, it would be a serious error to wait for further deterioration.

'...appropriate...to receive medical treatment in hospital'
As the definition of mental disorder in the Act is so broad, this phrase acts as a vital counterbalance. For many mental disorders, treatment is

not essential and in any case would not require admission to hospital. The possibility of treating mental disorders in the community has particular relevance since the advent of Community Treatment Orders.

The question of whether a disorder is of a nature or degree that makes treatment in hospital appropriate is a matter for expert opinion. The wording allows for developments in the science and in the practice of medicine. New treatments will be developed and others discarded as ineffective.

The balance between community and hospital treatment has changed enormously over the last 50 years and will change further in response to social and economic factors as well as scientific developments. The Act is worded so as to accommodate such changes. The test will depend on a reasonable body of professional opinion, which will change as the profession's standards change.

Professional opinion is not and should not be the sole arbiter. The term 'appropriate' implies proportionality. The question of whether or not detention in hospital for treatment is a proportionate response to the risks associated with a mental disorder is ultimately one for lay rather than professional opinion.

Availability of appropriate medical treatment

Detention under the Act requires that appropriate treatment is available. For the purposes of the Act, medical treatment includes:

- Nursing;
- Psychological intervention;
- Specialist mental health habilitation, rehabilitation and care.

(Habilitation involves the development of new skills and abilities whereas rehabilitation is helping the recovery of lost skills and abilities.)

Medical treatment under the Act is for the purpose of alleviating, or preventing, a worsening of a mental disorder or one or more of its symptoms or manifestations.[1] The implication is that it cannot be applied to any aspect of personality or behaviour that is not part of a recognised mental disorder. The *Code of Practice* allows a wide interpretation of

---

[1] Mental Health Act 1983 Section 145(4).

symptoms and manifestations as 'thoughts, emotions, communication, behaviour and actions'.[2]

An important change from the original 1983 Act is the emphasis on the purpose of medical treatment rather than its outcome. It is not necessary to demonstrate that a particular result is likely to be achieved. Lest any doubt should remain, the *Code of Practice* states that medical treatment may be appropriate even if the particular mental disorder is likely to persist or get worse despite that treatment. Also, 'It should never be assumed that any disorders, or any patients, are inherently or inevitably untreatable.'[3]

The 'appropriate treatment test' is designed to ensure that detention for treatment occurs only when treatment is offered. The Act does not allow preventive detention. Treatment must actually be available to the patient in the hospital concerned; the theoretical availability of treatment is not sufficient.

Whether or not a particular treatment is appropriate depends on:

- The nature and degree of the patient's mental disorder;
- All other circumstances of the case.

In other words, the treatment should be clinically appropriate but also appropriate in a more general sense, considering the patient's life and circumstances as a whole.

The more general circumstances to be considered may include:

- Physical health or disabilities;
- Culture and ethnicity;
- Age;
- Gender, gender identity and sexual orientation;
- Location of the available treatment;
- Potential impact on the patient's family and other relationships;
- Potential impact on education and work;
- The consequences for the patient and others if not treated.

The list is not exhaustive. The general principle is that detention for

---

[2] Department of Health, *Code of Practice: Mental Health Act 1983* (2008) para: 6.5.
[3] Department of Health, *Code of Practice: Mental Health Act 1983* (2008) para: 6.6.

RISK

treatment ought to be an appropriate, sensible and proportionate response bearing in mind the mental disorder and other aspects of the patient's life. As many of the considerations are social rather than clinical, it is essential to follow the general principle of consulting with relatives and carers.

The views of the patient are important, but reluctance to cooperate with treatment in general or with a specific intervention does not make that treatment inappropriate. Depending on the circumstances of the case, therapy which requires cooperation may still be the appropriate treatment even if the patient does not wish to engage with it.

There is considerable room for discretion and judgement when deciding on whether treatment is appropriate. What is appropriate will vary greatly between patients and the decision should be tailored to suit the individual case. Medical treatment will generally have a more ambitious aim than merely to prevent worsening of a mental disorder, but in a minority of patients with persistent mental disorders the management of undesirable consequences may be a realistic goal of compulsory admission – and therefore appropriate.

'the health or safety of the patient'
The risks are to be considered broadly and include:

- Suicide;
- Self-harm;
- Self-neglect;
- Putting health or safety at risk.

The risks may be accidental, reckless or unintentional. They may also be deliberate, as in some cases of self-harm.

Following the principles outlined under 'Nature and degree', the assessment of risk depends on history and present mental state. Historical factors to be considered in relation to the nature of the disorder include:

- A previous decline in mental health in the absence of treatment;
- The patient's own skills and experience in managing their condition;
- Previous incidents of self-harm or self-neglect.

Risks to health include physical and mental health so long as the risk derives from mental disorder. So detention under the Act can be used to treat self-starvation in, for example, depression or anorexia; poor control of chronic disease such as diabetes; overdose or other deliberate self-harm; so long as the problem is caused by mental disorder. The Act cannot be used to treat physical problems unrelated to mental disorder.

'the protection of others'

The risks to others are to be considered broadly and include:

- Physical assault;
- Sexual assault;
- Threats;
- Neglect;
- Exploitation;
- Serious emotional harm.

Violence can be defined as actual, attempted or threatened physical harm that is deliberate and non-consensual. It includes fear-inducing behaviour, where threats may be implicit or directed at third parties. Harm to others encompasses psychological as well as physical harm, so assessment under the Act can legitimately consider the extent to which other persons are put in fear.

Violence is only one of the forms of harm to others that may be the basis for detention in hospital. Assessment under the Act is often concerned with harms resulting from reckless or negligent behaviour rather than intentional violence. However, most of the literature on risk assessment and management is concerned with risk of violence. Many of the principles apply to all forms of harm to others.

Risk assessment and management

Chapter 12 gives a detailed consideration of risk assessment and management. The Act assumes professionals will have an adequate level of training appropriate to the circumstances in which they work.

When considering the protection of others it will be necessary to take account of:

- The nature of the risk;
- The likelihood of harm;
- The severity of harm;
- The vulnerability of potential victims.

There is a trade-off between likelihood and severity of harm. It is reasonable to tolerate a significant probability of minor harm whereas even a small probability of severe harm would be intolerable.

In practical terms, the assessment of potential harm to others depends on two major factors:

- Present mental state and behaviour, including threats or stated intent;
- A history of putting other persons at risk.

The discussion of nature and degree of the mental disorder is relevant here. The commonest mistake in risk assessment is to place too much emphasis on the first dimension, the here and now as it appears from the mental state at interview, whilst neglecting the history.

General considerations in risk assessment

As the assessment of risk depends so much on the history, professionals need to become more sophisticated in dealing with historical information. It is important to consider:

- The source of the information;
- The reliability of any sources;
- Third-party protection of sources;
- Conflicting information.

Who can make an application for detention in hospital?

The application must be made by an Approved Mental Health Professional (AMHP) or the patient's Nearest Relative (see Chapter 4). The AMHP is almost always more appropriate than the Nearest Relative because of the AMHP's professional training and knowledge of local resources. Also, an application by the Nearest Relative may have a negative impact on his or her relationship with the patient.

Doctors who are approached directly by a Nearest Relative about making an application should advise:

- It is preferable for an AMHP to consider the need for compulsory admission and to make any such application;

- The Nearest Relative has the right to require a local social services authority (LSSA) to arrange for an AMHP to consider the case with a view to admitting the person to hospital (and they must give reasons in writing if an application is not made in these circumstances).

The role of Approved Mental Health Professionals

AMHPs bring a social perspective to bear on their independent decision as to whether or not there are alternatives to detention under the Act. They cannot be told by the LSSA or by anyone else whether or not to make an application, but are required to 'exercise their own judgement, based on social and medical evidence'.[4] The AMHP must interview the patient and may make an application for detention if, after considering all the circumstances, he or she decides:

- The statutory criteria are met; and

- Detention in hospital is the most appropriate way of providing the care and medical treatment the patient needs.

If the AMHP decides an application should be made, the next step is to decide whether it is necessary and proper for the AMHP to make the

---

[4] Department of Health, *Code of Practice: Mental Health Act 1983* (2008) para: 4.51.

application. If so, and having considered the views of the patient's relatives and all the circumstances, the AMHP must make the application.

The interview between the patient and the AMHP

- The patient must be given the opportunity to have another person (e.g. friend, relative or advocate) present throughout the interview and subsequent process.

- The AMHP should assist in securing that person's attendance unless the urgency of the case makes it inappropriate to do so.

- Patients should usually be able to speak to the AMHP alone. The exception is when the AMHP fears violence and should insist that another professional is present as well as taking other appropriate steps to ensure the interview is conducted safely.

- Patients should not be interviewed through a closed door or window except as a last resort where there is a risk of serious violence that cannot be managed by other means.

- Where access to the patient is denied but there is no immediate risk of harm to the patient or to others, the AMHP should consider applying for a warrant under Section 135 of the Act to allow the police to enter the premises.

- When intoxication with alcohol or drugs (illicit or prescribed) prevents a proper interview, the AMHP should wait until the effects wear off or make arrangements to return later. If the urgency of the case precludes waiting, the AMHP must base the assessment on the available information.

The AMHP should note the circumstances of the interview and make a record of any actions taken along with the reasons for taking them. Record-keeping is particularly important when the circumstances or actions taken are in any way out of the ordinary.

The AMHP and the Nearest Relative

Obligations
Subject to certain exceptions, the obligations are as follows:

- The AMHP must attempt to identify the patient's Nearest Relative as defined in Section 26 of the Act.

- When making an application for detention under Section 2, the AMHP must take all practical steps to inform the Nearest Relative of the application and of the Nearest Relative's power to discharge the patient.

- The AMHP must consult the Nearest Relative before making an application for detention under Section 3 unless it is not reasonably practicable or would involve unreasonable delay.[5]

Exceptions

The exceptions are as follows:

- When it is not practicable for the AMHP to determine the identity or whereabouts of the Nearest Relative or the process would involve unreasonable delay.

- When the Nearest Relative's own health or mental capacity are impaired to an extent that makes consultation impossible.

- When informing or consulting the Nearest Relative would have a detrimental impact and infringe the patient's right to respect for his/her privacy and family life under Article 8 of the European Convention on Human Rights, unless justified by the benefit of involving the Nearest Relative.[6] Relevant cases are those in which the patient is likely to suffer emotional distress, damage to his/her mental health, physical harm, or financial or other exploitation as a result of the consultation. The context is usually one of previous abuse or exploitation by the Nearest Relative.

The obligation to consult and notify the Nearest Relative is a safeguard for the patient, so the exceptions should not be used lightly. Consultation must never be avoided simply because the Nearest Relative might object to the application. Before deciding not to inform and/or consult, the AMHP should consider all the circumstances of the case including:

---

[5] Department of Health, *Code of Practice: Mental Health Act 1983* (2008) para: 4.58.
[6] Department of Health, *Code of Practice: Mental Health Act 1983* (2008) para: 4.60 and see *R. (on the application of E) v Bristol City Council* [2005] EWHC 74 (Admin).

- The benefit to the patient of the Nearest Relative's involvement;

- The patient's wishes (taking account of current capacity to make the decision and any Advance Statement the patient may have made);

- Any detrimental effect the Nearest Relative's involvement may have on the patient's health and wellbeing;

- Whether there is reason to believe the patient's objection is intended to prevent the discovery of relevant information;

- The Nearest Relative's willingness to be involved on previous occasions, although unwillingness to act previously does not automatically imply current unwillingness.

Whenever the AMHP decides not to consult or inform the Nearest Relative, the reasons for the decision should be carefully recorded.

The purpose of consultation with the Nearest Relative

The AMHP should:

- Ascertain the Nearest Relative's views about both the patient's needs and the Nearest Relative's own needs in relation to the patient;

- Tell the Nearest Relative why an application is being considered and what the effects of such an application would be;

- Inform the Nearest Relative of his/her role and rights under the Act.

If the Nearest Relative objects to an application for detention under Section 3, the application cannot be made. If it is necessary to proceed with the application because of risks to the patient or to others, but the Nearest Relative cannot be persuaded to agree, the AMHP should consider applying to the County Court for the Nearest Relative's displacement under Section 29 of the Act.

For further discussion about the role and identity of the Nearest Nelative see chapter 5.

Consultation with other people

Although the Act mandates consultation only with the Nearest Relative, it is often useful and good practice to involve other people in decision- making. Carers, family members and friends are often well placed to provide additional information about the patient's history and circumstances. Depending on the degree of urgency, the AMHP should always consider whether to consult other carers, relatives or friends.

This is a sensitive area and when deciding whether it is appropriate to consult carers, relations or friends, the AMHP should consider:

- The patient's wishes;
- The nature of the relationship, including its length;
- Any evidence of hostility, abuse or exploitation.

The AMHP should also consult others involved with the patient's care, including people working for statutory, voluntary or independent services, such as substance misuse services, hostel staff or day centre workers.

When the patient is under 18, the AMHP should consider consulting with the patient's parents (or others who have parental responsibility) if the person concerned is not the Nearest Relative.

Note: The Mental Capacity Act
The patient may have an attorney appointed under a Lasting Power of Attorney or deputy appointed by the Court of Protection under the Mental Capacity Act, with authority to make decisions about the patient's personal welfare. In such a case, the AMHP should take reasonable steps to consult.

Where attorneys or deputies have the power to consent or refuse treatment for mental disorder on the patient's behalf, they should also be given the opportunity to talk directly to the doctors assessing the patient.[7]

---

[7] Department of Health, *Code of Practice: Mental Health Act 1983* (2008) para: 4.70.

Medical support for the application for detention

The application for detention must be supported by two medical recommendations. At least one of the doctors must be approved under Section 12 of the Act.

Where practicable, at least one of the doctors must have previous acquaintance with the patient. Preferably, the doctor should have treated the patient but it is sufficient to have had knowledge of the case. Similarly, it is preferable but not mandatory that the doctor without previous acquaintance with the patient should be approved under Section 12 of the Act.[8]

The medical examination

The medical examination must involve personal examination of the patient and his or her mental state as well as consideration of all available, relevant clinical information. Relevant clinical information includes that from both professional and non-professional sources.

If access to the patient is not immediately possible and it is not desirable to postpone the examination in order to negotiate access, consideration should be given to requesting that an AMHP apply for a warrant under Section 135 of the Act. Doctors must give reasons to support their opinions and they should include reference to symptoms and behaviour rather than simply to a diagnostic label.

The objectives of the assessment
The two objectives of the assessment are to determine whether:

- There are alternative means of safely providing care and treatment; and

- The criteria for detention are met.

Other practicalities

If doctors decide on admission to hospital, it is their responsibility to identify a suitable hospital bed. It is not the responsibility of the applicant,

---

[8] Department of Health, *Code of Practice: Mental Health Act 1983* (2008) para: 4.74.

unless it has been agreed locally between the LSSA and the relevant NHS bodies that this task will be done by any AMHP involved in the assessment.[9]

For detention under Section 3, doctors must state that appropriate medical treatment is available, which implies knowledge of the hospital to which the patient will be admitted. The doctor is therefore required to state the name of the hospital or, if there is uncertainty about where the bed will be, to list the acceptable possibilities.

In the case of highly specialised treatment, such as psychological treatment for severe personality disorder, it will be necessary to specify the particular unit or service.

Section 2 or Section 3?

Section 2 of the Act should be used if there is uncertainty about:

- The precise nature or degree of a patient's mental disorder;
- The treatment plan;
- Whether the patient is likely to accept treatment voluntarily following admission;
- Availability of appropriate treatment.

There should be a reasonable expectation that a brief compulsory admission will allow the uncertainty to be resolved. Section 2 can be used in patients undergoing treatment if there is a need for admission in order to re-assess or to re-formulate a treatment plan.

Difficulty in finding a suitable bed for a patient, who might otherwise be admitted under Section 3, amounts to uncertainty about the availability of appropriate treatment. It is therefore a legitimate reason for admission under Section 2.

The requirement to identify a hospital or hospitals when detaining a patient under Section 3 is an important change to the 1983 Act. It is no longer possible to detain the patient, then begin the search for a bed, because detention requires that appropriate treatment is available.

---

[9] Department of Health, *Code of Practice: Mental Health Act 1983* (2008) para: 4.75.

Section 3 must be used if the patient is already detained under Section 2, because a new Section 2 application cannot be made in such circumstances. Section 3 should also be used when the following are established:

- The nature and degree of the patient's mental disorder;
- The essential elements of the treatment plan;
- It is unlikely that the patient will accept treatment voluntarily after a brief admission;
- Appropriate treatment is available, including availability of a hospital place.

Renewal of authority for detention

The procedures for renewing detention and extending Supervised Community Treatment (SCT) are the same. The criteria for renewal of authority for detention or for extending SCT are the same as the criteria for making the orders.

The Responsible Clinicians (RC) must examine the patient and within the two months leading up to expiry of the order for detention:

- Decide whether criteria for renewal are met and if so:
- Consult at least one other person who has been professionally concerned with the patient's treatment, and obtain the written agreement of 'the second professional' that the criteria are met. The second professional must not belong to the same profession as the Responsible Clinician; and
- Submit a report to the Hospital Managers.

The second professional
The involvement of a second professional is intended as a safeguard for patients by ensuring renewal is formally agreed by two suitably qualified and competent professionals who:

- Are familiar with the patient's case;
- Are from different disciplines;
- Make independent decisions.

The second professional should:

- Have sufficient experience and expertise to make the decision;
- Have been actively involved in the planning, management or delivery of the patient's treatment;
- Have had sufficient recent contact with the patient to be able to make an informed judgement;
- Satisfy themselves they have sufficient information on which to base a decision (which may or may not require a separate interview with the patient depending on previous contact).

There is no requirement for the second professional to be an Approved Clinician.

Beyond these requirements, the Act does not specify who can act as a second professional. Hospital Managers should determine local policy based on the principle of providing an additional safeguard for patients in the form of a second opinion with a different but complementary professional perspective from that of the Responsible Clinician.

- The Responsible Clinician should record the identity of the second professional before examining the patient to decide on renewal.
- The decision of the second professional must be accepted unless there are exceptional circumstances.
- In exceptional circumstances, the Responsible Clinician may seek the agreement of a different second professional.
- These exceptional circumstances should be drawn to the attention of the Hospital Managers when a renewal report is made.

Discharge: the powers of the Responsible Clinician

The Responsible Clinician can discharge most detained patients by giving an order in writing.

Criteria for detention/renewal must be kept under review and the patient discharged if at any time the criteria are not met.

Discharge: the powers of the Nearest Relative

The Nearest Relative can discharge a patient detained for assessment or treatment under Part 2 of the Act, but conditions apply:

- The Nearest Relative must give the Hospital Managers at least 72 hours' notice in writing of his/her intention to discharge the patient.

- During that period, the Responsible Clinician can block the discharge by issuing a 'barring report' stating that, if discharged, the patient is likely to act in a manner dangerous to self or others.

- The issue centres on the specific risks of serious physical injury or lasting psychological harm, not merely on a general need for safety or the protection of others.

This is discussed in more detail in chapter 5.

Discharge: Hospital Managers and the Tribunal

This topic is discussed in chapter 6.

Chapter 3

Consent to Treatment

The topic of consent to treatment in detained patients has the potential to cause confusion because:

- Different criteria are used to determine liability to detention under the Act and lack of capacity to consent to treatment;

- Different rules apply to different treatments;

- There are some differences between detention under different sections of the Act.

There are also different rules which apply to consent to treatment for Supervised Community Treatment (SCT). These are considered in chapter 7.

Medical treatment: definitions

In the Act, 'medical treatment' also includes nursing, psychological intervention and specialist mental health habilitation, rehabilitation and care.

The Act defines medical treatment for mental disorder as: 'Medical treatment which is for the purpose of alleviating or preventing a worsening of a mental disorder or one or more of its symptoms or manifestations.'

The definition includes treatment of physical health problems only when such treatment is part of, or ancillary to, treatment for mental disorder (e.g. treatment of self-starvation or wounds self-inflicted as a result of mental disorder).[1] Outside this context the Act does not regulate medical treatment for physical health problems.

'Consent' is the voluntary and continuing permission of a patient to accept a treatment, based on sufficient knowledge of the purpose, nature, likely effects and risks of that treatment, including the likelihood of its success and any alternatives to it. Permission given under coercion (i.e. any unfair or undue pressure) is not consent because it is not truly voluntary.[2]

Treatments to which special rules and procedures apply

The situation is further complicated because within the broad definition of medical treatment for mental disorder there are treatments to which special rules apply. They are: medication after an initial three-month period; electro-convulsive therapy (ECT); neurosurgery; and implantation of hormones to reduce male sex drive. These treatments are considered in more detail in the latter part of this chapter.

Definition of 'detained patient'

In the following discussion a 'detained patient' is one who is liable to be detained in hospital under any section of the Act (including an SCT patient who has been recalled to hospital and a patient on leave of absence or absent without leave) with the following exceptions:

- A patient detained as an emergency under Section 4;
- A patient held under the holding powers in Section 5;
- A patient remanded to hospital for reports under Section 35;
- A patient detained in hospital as a place of safety under Sections 135 or 136;
- A patient temporarily detained in hospital as a place of safety under Section 37 or 45A pending admission to the hospital named in a hospital order or hospital direction;

---

[1] Department of Health, *Code of Practice: Mental Health Act 1983* (2008) para: 23.4.
[2] Department of Health, *Code of Practice: Mental Health Act 1983* (2008) para: 23.31.

- A conditionally discharged restricted patient.

The exceptions are in the same position as patients not subject to the Act; their rights to consent to or to refuse treatment are unchanged by their status under the Act. For the purposes of the following discussion they are not regarded as detained patients.

Another exceptional case is that of SCT patients not recalled to hospital, including SCT patients who have agreed to voluntary admission so are in hospital without having been recalled. Part 4A of the Act sets out the rules for their treatment (see chapter 7).

If Sections 57, 58 or 58A of the Act apply: a detained patient can be given the treatment only by following the rules and procedures set out in the Act (see below). Note that Section 57 also applies to patients who are not detained or otherwise subject to the Act; and Section 58A applies to all patients under the age of 18.

When Sections 57, 58 or 58A of the Act do not apply: Section 63 allows a detained patient to be given medical treatment for mental disorder if:

- The patient consents to the treatment;

- The patient does not consent but the treatment is given by or under the direction of the Approved Clinician in charge of the treatment.

Capacity and consent

The Act often requires a determination of:

- Whether a patient has the capacity to consent to or refuse a medical treatment; and

- if so, whether the patient does in fact consent.

The rules for answering these questions are the same as for any other patient and they are determined mainly by the Mental Capacity Act 2005 (see chapter 13 for a fuller discussion).

Capacity to consent: people aged 16 or over

For people aged 16 or over, capacity to consent is defined by the Mental Capacity Act (MCA). The following principles of the MCA are particularly relevant to the operation of the Mental Health Act:[3]

- A patient must be assumed to have capacity unless it is established that he or she lacks capacity;

- A patient may lack capacity to make a decision about one issue but not about others – the assessment has to be made in relation to the particular decision;

- A patient is not be to be treated as unable to make a decision unless all practicable steps to help him/her to do so have been taken without success; and

- A patient is not to be treated as unable to make a decision merely because he/she makes an unwise decision.

- Mental disorder does not necessarily mean a patient lacks capacity to give or refuse consent, or to take any other decision;

- Capacity can vary over time so it should be assessed when the decision in question needs to be taken;

- Where a patient's capacity fluctuates, there may be a case for delaying the decision until the patient has capacity, but in the case of medication for acute conditions the spontaneous recovery of capacity may be unlikely;

- Explanations should be appropriate to the level of the patient's assessed ability;

- All assessments of a patient's capacity should be fully recorded in his or her notes.

Competence to consent: children under 16

The MCA does not apply to medical treatment for children under 16. Children with sufficient understanding and intelligence to comprehend fully what is involved in a proposed treatment are considered competent (or 'Gillick competent') to consent to it. The common law deals with cases where children are not capable of consenting.[4]

---

[3] Department of Health, *Code of Practice: Mental Health Act 1983* (2008) paras: 23.28 & 23.29.
[4] Department of Health, *Code of Practice: Mental Health Act 1983* (2008) para: 23.30.

General principles of consent to treatment

By definition, a person who lacks capacity to consent cannot consent to treatment. Professionals have a duty to provide adequate information when seeking consent; and to continue to provide information about the proposed treatment and alternatives. 'Adequate information' must relate to the particular patient, the particular treatment and relevant clinical knowledge and practice.

In every case, sufficient information must be given to the patient to ensure he or she understands in broad terms the nature, likely effects and all significant possible adverse outcomes of that treatment, including the likelihood of its success and any alternatives to it. A record should be kept of information provided to patients.

The patient should be invited to ask questions and the answers should be full, frank and truthful.

There may sometimes be a compelling reason, in the patient's interests, for not disclosing certain information. A professional who chooses not to disclose information must be prepared to justify the decision. A professional who chooses not to answer a patient's question should make this clear to the patient so that the patient knows where he or she stands.

Patients should be told their consent to treatment can be withdrawn at any time.

When patients withdraw their consent (or are considering withdrawing it), they should be given a clear explanation of the likely consequences of not receiving the treatment and (where relevant) the circumstances in which the treatment may be given without their consent under the Mental Health Act.

A record should be kept of the information provided to patients.

Treatment without consent – general points

Although the Act permits some medical treatment to be given without consent, the clinician should seek the patient's consent when possible. The patient's consent or refusal should be recorded in the notes along with an assessment of the patient's capacity to consent.

If a patient consents but later withdraws consent, or loses the capacity to consent, the treatment must be reviewed. The clinician must decide whether to proceed in the absence of consent; to provide alternative treatment; or to cease treatment.

A clinician authorising or administering treatment without consent under the Mental Health Act performs a function of a public nature and is therefore subject to the provisions of the Human Rights Act 1998. It is unlawful for the clinician to act in a way which is incompatible with a patient's rights as set out in the European Convention on Human Rights ('the Convention').[5]

The *Code of Practice* draws attention to the following:[6] compulsory administration of treatment which would otherwise require consent is invariably an infringement of Article 8 of the Convention (respect for family and private life) but it may be justified:

- If it is in accordance with law (in this case the Mental Health Act); and

- If it is proportionate to a legitimate aim (in this case, the reduction of the risk posed by a person's mental disorder and the improvement of his/her health).

If its effects are severe, compulsory treatment may amount to inhuman treatment or even torture contrary to Article 3 of the Convention. However, the European Court of Human Rights has said that a measure which is shown to be of therapeutic necessity according to established principles of medicine cannot in principle be regarded as inhuman and degrading.

Treatment plans

A patient's Responsible Clinician must ensure that the patient has a treatment plan. The treatment plan should:

- Form part of a care plan under the Care Programme Approach (see page 123) or its equivalent;

---

[5] Department of Health, *Code of Practice: Mental Health Act 1983* (2008) para: 23.39.
[6] Department of Health, *Code of Practice: Mental Health Act 1983* (2008) para: 23.40.

- Be recorded in the patient's notes;

- Include a description of the immediate and long-term goals for the patient;

- Give a clear indication of the treatments proposed and the methods of treatment.[7]

When possible, the treatment plan should be discussed with the patient and, subject to considerations of patient confidentiality, with the patient's carers so they can contribute and express their views. When a patient cannot or does not wish to participate in discussion about a treatment plan, the clinician should take into consideration any views the patient has expressed in the past.

Treatment plans should be regularly reviewed and the results of reviews recorded in the patient's notes.[8]

Interface between Parts 4 and 4A of the Mental Health Act and Section 28 of the Mental Capacity Act

Treatments to which special rules and procedures apply

Sections 57, 58 and 58A of the Act specify the treatments for mental disorder to which special rules and procedures apply.

Summary of treatments covered by Sections 57, 58 and 58A[9]

Section	Treatment
Section 57	Neurosurgery for mental disorder Surgical implantation of hormones to reduce male sex drive
Section 58	Medication (after an initial three-month period) – except medication administered as part of electro-convulsive therapy (ECT)
Section 58A	ECT and medication administered as part of ECT

---

[7] Department of Health, *Code of Practice: Mental Health Act 1983* (2008) paras: 23.42-23.46.
[8] Department of Health, *Code of Practice: Mental Health Act 1983* (2008) para: 23.51.
[9] Department of Health, *Code of Practice: Mental Health Act 1983* (2008) para: 23.6.

In most cases the special procedure is a requirement for a certificate of approval from a Second Opinion Appointed Doctor (SOAD).

Definitions[10]

SOAD: a doctor appointed by the Care Quality Commission to give a second opinion regarding approval of certain forms of treatment;

SOAD certificate: a certificate issued by a SOAD approving treatment for a particular patient;

Part 4A patient: a patient subject to Supervised Community Treatment (SCT) who has not been recalled to hospital; and

Part 4A certificate: a SOAD certificate issued under Part 4A of the Act in respect of the treatment of an SCT patient.

Clinician in charge of treatment: the clinician in charge of the treatment in question, who need not be the Responsible Clinician in charge of a patient's case overall. For example, the Responsible Clinician may be a psychologist but the clinician in charge of drug therapy would be a medical doctor, or vice versa.

Approved Clinician
Hospital managers are required to keep a record of Approved Clinicians and should ensure that Approved Clinicians are in charge of treatment where the Act requires it.

The clinician in charge of treatment must be an Approved Clinician when treatment is given to a detained patient under any of the following conditions:[11]

- Without the patient's consent;

- With the patient's consent on the basis of a certificate issued under Section 58 or 58A by an Approved Clinician (rather than a SOAD);

- Continued with the consent of an SCT patient who has been recalled to hospital (including one whose community treatment order has then been revoked) to avoid serious suffering to the patient;

---

[10] Department of Health, *Code of Practice: Mental Health Act 1983* (2008) para: 24.2.
[11] Department of Health, *Code of Practice: Mental Health Act 1983* (2008) para: 24.4.

- In a Part 4A patient who lacks capacity to consent to it and without the consent of an attorney, deputy or the Court of Protection (unless it is immediately necessary and being given under Section 64G).

Treatments requiring consent and a second opinion under Section 57

Section 57 applies to:

- Neurosurgery for mental disorder; and
- Surgical implantation of hormones to reduce male sex drive.

It applies to these treatments in any and all patients whether or not they are otherwise subject to the Act.

Where Section 57 applies, these treatments can be given only if all the following requirements are met:

- The patient consents to the treatment;
- A SOAD and two other people nominated by the Commission certify that the patient has the capacity to consent and has done so; and
- The SOAD certifies that it is appropriate for the treatment to be given to the patient.

A certificate issued by the SOAD immediately becomes ineffective if the patient no longer consents to the treatment or if the patient loses the capacity to consent to the treatment.

Most mental health professionals will get through their careers without ever being directly involved in either of these treatments; they are rare procedures likely to be provided only by specialist centres. Such hospitals should agree with the Commission the procedures they will follow to ensure compliance with the requirements of Section 57.

Treatments requiring consent or a second opinion under Section 58

Section 58 applies to medication for mental disorder but only when three months have passed from the day on which any medication for mental

disorder was first given to the patient during the current period of detention under the Act ('the three-month period'). Section 58 does not apply
to medication administered as part of electro-convulsive therapy (ECT),
which is covered by Section 58A.

Detained patients can be given medication to which Section 58 applies
only when:

- The Approved Clinician in charge of the treatment, or a SOAD,
  certifies that the patient has the capacity to consent and has done
  so; or

- A SOAD certifies the treatment is appropriate even though the
  patient is non-consenting.

As always, a non-consenting patient either lacks the capacity to consent or
has the capacity to consent but does not consent.

The *Code of Practice* requires Hospital Managers to have in place systems
to remind the clinician in charge of the medication and the patient at least
four weeks before the expiry of the three-month period.[12]

Where Approved Clinicians certify the treatment of a patient who
consents, they should make a record in the patient's notes of the reasons
for believing the patient has consented to the treatment.[13]

Certificates under Section 58 must set out the specific treatments to which
they apply:[14]

- List all relevant drugs including medication to be given 'as
  required' (prn).

- Identify drugs by name or by the classes described in the *British
  National Formulary* (*BNF*).

- If drugs are specified by class, state clearly the number of drugs
  authorised in each class and whether any drugs in the class are
  excluded.

- Indicate the route of administration and maximum dosage for
  each drug or category of drugs.

---

[12] Department of Health, *Code of Practice: Mental Health Act 1983* (2008) para: 24.14.
[13] Department of Health, *Code of Practice: Mental Health Act 1983* (2008) para: 24.16.
[14] Department of Health, *Code of Practice: Mental Health Act 1983* (2008) para: 24.17.

- Maximum dosage may be specified for a drug or class as 'within *BNF* limits'.

- It is also permissible to specify doses in excess of the range given in the *BNF*. Care is needed and reasons should be clearly stated in the clinical notes.

A certificate issued by an Approved Clinician under Section 58 ceases to be effective when the clinician concerned stops being the Approved Clinician in charge of the treatment.

A SOAD certificate under Section 58 ceases to be effective when:[15]

- The patient stops (even if only temporarily) being either a detained patient or an SCT patient.

- Any time limit placed on approval of treatment expires.

- The certificate was given on the basis that the patient consented, but the patient no longer consents or has lost the capacity to consent.

- The certificate was given on the basis that the patient lacked capacity to consent, but the patient now has that capacity.

- The certificate was given on the basis that the patient had capacity to consent but was refusing, and either the patient is now consenting or the patient has lost the capacity to consent.

Electro-convulsive therapy (ECT) under Section 58A

For now, Section 58A applies only to ECT and to medication administered as part of ECT. Other treatments may be included under the Section in the future. Section 58A applies to detained patients and to all patients under 18 whether or not they are detained.

- A detained patient who has the capacity to consent may be given ECT only with his/her consent. The clinician in charge or a SOAD must certify that the patient has the capacity to consent and has done so.

- A patient aged under 18 years can be given ECT only when a SOAD has certified the treatment is appropriate. The SOAD certificate is sufficient in a detained patient but in all other cases

---

[15] Department of Health, *Code of Practice: Mental Health Act 1983* (2008) para: 24.79.

the clinician must also have the patient's consent or other legal authority to treat.

- A patient who lacks the capacity to consent may be given ECT only if a SOAD certifies all the following:

    – that the patient lacks capacity to consent; that the treatment is appropriate;

    – that no valid and applicable Advance Decision has been made by the patient under the Mental Capacity Act 2005 (MCA), refusing the treatment;

    – that no suitably authorised attorney or deputy objects to the treatment on the patient's behalf; and

    – that the treatment would not conflict with a decision of the Court of Protection which prevents the treatment being given.

In all cases the SOAD should indicate on the certificate the maximum number of administrations of ECT that may be given.

A certificate issued by an Approved Clinician under Section 58A ceases to be effective when the clinician concerned stops being the Approved Clinician in charge of the treatment. In addition, a SOAD certificate under Section 58A ceases to be effective when:[16]

- The patient stops (even if only temporarily) being either a detained patient or an SCT patient (except for patients aged under 18).

- Any time limit on approval (if specified) expires.

- The certificate was given on the basis that the patient consented, but the patient no longer consents or has lost the capacity to consent.

- The certificate was given on the basis that the patient had capacity to consent but was refusing, and either the patient is now consenting or the patient has lost the capacity to consent.

- The certificate was given on the understanding that the treatment would not conflict with an Advance Decision to refuse

---

[16] Department of Health, *Code of Practice: Mental Health Act 1983* (2008) para: 24.79.

treatment, but the person giving the treatment becomes aware that there is such a conflict.

- The certificate was given on the understanding that the treatment would not conflict with a decision of an attorney, a deputy, or the Court of Protection, but the person giving the treatment becomes aware that there is such a conflict; or an attorney, deputy, or the Court of Protection makes a new decision that the treatment should not be given.

The conditions imposed by Section 58A are a reminder of the public anxiety surrounding this form of treatment. Whether or not the Act applies, all patients who receive ECT should be given written information before treatment to assist them in understanding the nature, purpose and likely effects of the treatment.

Part 4A certificates

Part 4A patients may be given certain treatments for mental disorder only if a SOAD has certified that the treatment is appropriate. A Part 4A certificate is needed for:[17]

- Treatment which would require a certificate under Section 58 if the patient were detained (i.e. medication after the three-month limit). However, a certificate is not required during the first month following a patient's discharge from detention onto SCT (even if the three-month period has expired or expires during that first month); and

- ECT or other treatments to which Section 58A may apply in the future.

The Part 4A certificate need not comment on capacity or consent. The SOAD may make it a condition of approval that particular treatments are given only in certain circumstances, including a condition that a particular treatment be given only with the patient's consent. For example, the SOAD may specify that a medication may be given up to a certain dosage if the patient lacks capacity to consent, but that a higher dosage

---

[17] Department of Health, *Code of Practice: Mental Health Act 1983* (2008) para: 24.26.

may be given with the patient's consent.[18]

The Part 4A certificate ceases to be effective when:

- The patient stops (even if only temporarily) being either a detained patient or an SCT patient.

- The SOAD specified a time limit on the approval of a course of treatment, and the time limit has expired.

SCT patients recalled to hospital – exceptions to the need for certificates under Section 58 or 58A

SCT patients recalled to hospital are subject to Sections 58 and 58A in the same way as other detained patients with three exceptions:[19]

- A certificate under Section 58 is not needed for medication if less than one month has passed since the patient was discharged from hospital and became an SCT patient;

- No certificate is needed under Sections 58 or 58A if the treatment is authorised for administration on recall on the patient's Part 4A certificate;

- Treatment that was already being given under a Part 4A certificate may be continued if the Approved Clinician considers that discontinuation would cause the patient serious suffering even though the treatment was not authorised for administration on recall. The treatment may be continued only pending compliance with Section 58 or 58A (as applicable) – that is, whilst steps are being taken to obtain a new certificate.

When giving Part 4A certificates a SOAD needs to consider what (if any) treatments to approve should the patient be recalled to hospital and whether to impose any conditions on that approval. Unless the SOAD specifies otherwise, the Part 4A certificate will authorise the treatment even if the patient has capacity to refuse it (except in the case of ECT

---

[18] Department of Health, *Code of Practice: Mental Health Act 1983* (2008) para: 24.27.
[19] Department of Health, *Code of Practice: Mental Health Act 1983* (2008) para: 24.28.

or other Section 58A type treatment).[20] The potential advantage is that treatments can be given quickly after recall without the need to obtain a new certificate.

Urgent cases (Sections 62, 64B, 64C and 64E)

Section 62 allows for exceptions to the requirements for a certificate under Sections 57, 58 and 58A in urgent cases where treatment is immediately necessary. Sections 64B, 64C and 64E serve the same function in relation to SCT and set out the conditions under which a Part 4A certificate is not required when treatment is immediately necessary. These exceptions apply only if the treatment is immediately necessary to:

- Save the patient's life;

- Prevent serious deterioration of the patient's condition, and the treatment does not have unfavourable physical or psychological consequences which cannot be reversed;

- Alleviate serious suffering by the patient, and the treatment does not have unfavourable physical or psychological consequences which cannot be reversed and does not entail significant physical hazard; or

- Prevent the patient behaving violently or being a danger to him/herself or others, and the treatment represents the minimum interference necessary for that purpose, does not have unfavourable physical or psychological consequences which cannot be reversed and does not entail significant physical hazard.

Only the first two categories apply when the treatment is ECT – that is, it can only be given as urgent treatment when it is immediately necessary to save life or to prevent serious deterioration.

Urgent treatment under these Sections can continue only for as long as it remains immediately necessary.

Although certificates are not required where treatment is immediately necessary, the other requirements of Parts 4 and 4A of the Act still apply.[21]

---

[20] Department of Health, *Code of Practice: Mental Health Act 1983* (2008) para: 24.29.
[21] Department of Health, *Code of Practice: Mental Health Act 1983* (2008) para: 24.36.

The role of the SOAD

The SOAD provides an additional safeguard for patients by deciding whether certain treatments are appropriate and issuing certificates accordingly. Although appointed by the Care Quality Commission, SOADs act as independent professionals and must reach their own judgement about whether the proposed treatment is appropriate.[22]

The SOAD's decision on a particular treatment must take into account both the clinical appropriateness of the treatment and its more general appropriateness in the light of all other circumstances.

The SOAD should:

- Consider alternative treatments to that proposed;
- Balance potential benefits of the treatment against its negative effects;
- Try to understand the patient's views and the reasoning behind them;
- Take account of the patient's views and preferences;
- Take account of the patient's previous experience of treatment;
- Take account of the opinions, knowledge, experience and skills of other persons consulted.

Requesting a SOAD visit

The clinician in charge of the treatment in question has personal responsibility for ensuring a request is made to the Commission for a SOAD to visit. Clinicians should not ask a SOAD to issue a certificate they, the clinicians, could provide themselves – that is, confirming consent to treatment. The clinician should ask the SOAD for an opinion only when the clinician is unable to decide the issue.[23]

Arranging and preparing for SOAD visits

The SOAD visits detained patients in hospital.

---

[22] Department of Health, *Code of Practice: Mental Health Act 1983* (2008) para: 24.56.
[23] Department of Health, *Code of Practice: Mental Health Act 1983* (2008) para: 24.39.

For SCT patients, Hospital Managers should ensure arrangements are made for the SOAD to see the patient at a mutually agreed place – for example, at an outpatient clinic.

Attending hospital for examination by a SOAD is a condition of all SCT, so if a patient fails to attend when asked to do so he/she may be recalled to hospital for the examination if necessary. However, recall should be a last resort.[24]

The treatment proposal for the patient, together with notes of any relevant multi-disciplinary discussion on which it was based, must be given to the SOAD before or at the time of the visit.

If a Part 4A certificate is being requested, the proposal should clearly indicate which (if any) treatments it is proposed should be authorised in the case of recall to hospital.

The SOAD visit

During a visit the SOAD should:[25]

- Check the patient's detention or SCT papers are in order; and
- Interview the patient in private if possible. Others may be present if the patient and the SOAD wish or to manage any risk of physical harm from the patient if the SOAD agrees that the measure is necessary.

Hospital Managers are responsible for ensuring that:

- All relevant documentation, including full clinical notes, is available;
- People whom the SOAD wishes to meet (including the clinician in charge of the treatment) are available when the SOAD visits.

The SOAD has a right to access records without the patient's consent if necessary, but that right is limited to records relating to treatment in the hospital or other establishment in which the SOAD examines the patient. That fact may influence the choice of venue for the examination when the patient refuses consent for access to records.

---

[24] Department of Health, *Code of Practice: Mental Health Act 1983* (2008) para: 24.41.
[25] Department of Health, *Code of Practice: Mental Health Act 1983* (2008) para: 24.43.

Approved Clinicians should ensure the SOAD is informed if the patient has an attorney or deputy who is authorised under the MCA to make decisions about medical treatment on the patient's behalf. Details of relevant Advance Decisions, or Advance Statements of views, wishes or feelings, should be drawn to the SOAD's attention.[26]

Statutory consultees

The SOAD is required to consult two people before issuing a certificate approving treatment. The Act does not specify who they should be. They should have knowledge of the patient and be able to help inform the decision as to whether the proposed treatment is appropriate.

- Both statutory consultees must have been professionally concerned with the patient's medical treatment;

- Neither may be the clinician in charge of the proposed treatment or the Responsible Clinician;

- One must be a nurse;

- The other must be neither a nurse nor a doctor.

Statutory consultees should expect to have a private discussion with the SOAD and should consider commenting on:[27]

- The proposed treatment and the patient's ability to consent to it;

- Their understanding of the past and present views and wishes of the patient;

- Other treatment options and the way in which the decision on the treatment proposal was arrived at;

- The patient's progress and the views of the patient's carers;

- The implications of imposing treatment on a reluctant patient who does not want it and the reasons why the patient is refusing treatment.

A proposed statutory consultee who feels unable to carry out the role should inform the clinician in charge and the SOAD as soon as possible.

---

[26] Department of Health, *Code of Practice: Mental Health Act 1983* (2008) para: 24.48.

[27] Department of Health, *Code of Practice: Mental Health Act 1983* (2008) para: 24.52.

A SOAD should be prepared (when appropriate and subject to the patient's agreement) to consult a wider range of people concerned with the patient's care than those required by the Act – for example, the patient's GP, Nearest Relative, family, carers, and any Independent Mental Health Advocate or other advocate representing the patient.

The SOAD's decision and reasons

The SOAD must provide written reasons in support of a decision to approve treatments. These may be recorded on the certificate or given to the clinician in charge of the treatment as soon as possible afterwards.

The clinician may act on the certificate before receiving the SOAD's reasons but if there is no urgency to treat it is preferable to wait for them, especially if the patient is likely to be unhappy with the decision.[28]

The clinician in charge of the treatment has a personal responsibility to communicate the results of the SOAD visit to the patient. When a separate statement of reasons is received, the patient should be given the opportunity to see it as soon as possible unless the clinician or the SOAD believe it would be likely to cause serious harm to the physical or mental health of the patient or any other person.[29]

The clinician and the SOAD should make every attempt to reach agreement. If the SOAD is unable to agree with the clinician in charge of the treatment he/she should inform the clinician personally as soon as possible and give reasons for the disagreement.

The opinion given by the SOAD is the SOAD's personal responsibility and there can be no appeal to the Commission against it.

Status of certificates under Part 4 and Part 4A

Original signed certificates should be kept with the documents which authorise the patient's detention or SCT. Copies should be kept:

- In the patient's notes;

---

[28] Department of Health, *Code of Practice: Mental Health Act 1983* (2008) para: 24.60.
[29] Department of Health, *Code of Practice: Mental Health Act 1983* (2008) para: 24.62.

- With the patient's prescription chart if the certificate concerns medication.[30]

Review of treatment and withdrawal of approval (Sections 61 and 64H)

The Act does not require the validity of certificates to be reviewed after any particular period but it is good practice to review them at regular intervals.

The clinician in charge of any treatment given in accordance with a SOAD certificate must provide a written report on that treatment and the relevant patient's condition at any time if requested to do so by the Commission under Section 61 or 64H of the Act. The report should be copied to the patient.[31]

Under Sections 61 and 64H, the Commission may at any time direct that a certificate is no longer to approve some or all of the treatments specified in it. When the Commission revokes approval, treatment which is already in progress may continue, pending a new certificate, if the clinician in charge of it considers that discontinuation would cause the patient serious suffering.[32]

The exception applies only whilst steps are taken to obtain a new certificate. It cannot be used to continue treatment under Section 57 or Section 58A against the wishes of a patient with capacity because in those cases it would be impossible to obtain a new certificate.[33]

When treatment is continued to avoid serious suffering pending compliance with a certificate requirement, the clinician should immediately take steps to ask for a SOAD visit. If the SOAD visits and decides not to give a certificate, the treatment must end immediately.

As with immediately necessary treatment given without a certificate, Hospital Managers are required to monitor the use of these exceptions.[34]

---

[30] Department of Health, *Code of Practice: Mental Health Act 1983* (2008) para: 24.71.
[31] Department of Health, *Code of Practice: Mental Health Act 1983* (2008) para: 24.73.
[32] Department of Health, *Code of Practice: Mental Health Act 1983* (2008) para: 24.75.
[33] Department of Health, *Code of Practice: Mental Health Act 1983* (2008) para: 24.76.
[34] Department of Health, *Code of Practice: Mental Health Act 1983* (2008) para: 24.78.

Chapter 4

Professional Roles

The Mental Health Act 1983 establishes a number of professional roles, which have specified functions and responsibilities under the Act. These professional roles are the Approved Clinician, the Responsible Clinician, Section 12 doctors, the Approved Mental Health Professional, Guardians, and Hospital Managers. This chapter considers each of these in turn. It also considers the new role of Independent Mental Health Advocate, which is then covered in greater detail in the next chapter.

Approved Clinician

Definition

An Approved Clinician is a mental health professional who is approved by the Secretary of State (or the Welsh Ministers), although in practice this function is delegated to Strategic Health Authorities, Primary Care Trusts and Health Boards.

Under the Mental Health Act 1983 Approved Clinicians (General) Directions 2008 only the following professionals may be approved:

- Registered medical practitioners;

- Chartered psychologists;

- Registered first level nurses whose field of practice is mental health nursing or learning disabilities nursing;

- Registered occupational therapists; and

- Social workers registered with the General Social Care Council.

Some decisions under the Act can be taken only by an Approved Clinician. Only an Approved Clinician is eligible to be a Responsible Clinician.

Responsible Clinician

The 2007 revision abolished the medical role of Responsible Medical Officer and replaced it with the role of Responsible Clinician (RC), who need not be a doctor. The Responsible Clinician (RC) is the Approved Clinician with overall responsibility for the patient's care.

Only the Responsible Clinician may:

- Renew an order for detention; or

- Place a patient on Supervised Community Treatment (SCT).

Allocating or changing the Responsible Clinician

Allocation

Hospital Managers are required to develop local protocols for allocating Responsible Clinicians to patients. In order to do that they must keep a register of Approved Clinicians within their services.

The issue of allocation of Responsible Clinician is most likely to arise at times of transition when a patient moves between hospitals, between services, or from hospital to the community.

Life was simpler in the past because the Responsible Medical Officer was usually the patient's consultant. The 2007 revision opens up a range of possibilities and should facilitate better treatment. The guiding principle is:

- the Responsible Clinician should be the Approved Clinician with the skills and expertise most appropriate to the patient's needs (see *Code of Practice* para: 14.3).

If, for example, a patient's treatment is mainly psychological, it may be most appropriate to appoint a psychologist as the Responsible Clinician.

If medication is the mainstay of treatment, the Responsible Clinician will usually be a doctor. Note, however, that the term 'appropriate' is used here, as in other parts of the Act, to mean both clinically appropriate and more generally appropriate in all the circumstances. Factors bearing on the choice of Responsible Clinician may therefore include:

- The views of the patient;
- The views of carers or relatives;
- Preference for a clinician of a specific gender;
- Anything else of relevance bearing in mind the guiding principles of the Act.

A patient subject to the Act must always have a Responsible Clinician. If there is uncertainty about which Approved Clinician is most appropriate, the choice must be based on what is known about the patient's needs at the time. The Responsible Clinician can be changed later if necessary, but there cannot be a delay in allocation.

The Responsible Clinician can be selected only from the pool of Approved Clinicians available within a particular service. The Approved Clinician must be 'good enough' to take on the role of Responsible Clinician in a particular case. In the case of children and young people, the Responsible Clinician should be a specialist in the sub-specialty.

Local protocols must:

- Ensure the patient's Responsible Clinician is the available Approved Clinician with the skills and expertise best suited to the patient's needs;
- Ensure easy identification of the Responsible Clinician;
- Put in place cover arrangements;
- Make arrangements for ongoing review of the appropriateness of the Responsible Clinician to a particular patient's needs.

The ongoing review of appropriateness is necessary because a patient's needs may change with time. Whilst the Responsible Clinician should be the best person for the job there is also value in continuity of care so frequent changes should be avoided.

Specialist treatments

It will often be the case that the Responsible Clinician can oversee the patient's main needs for treatment and assessment but is not qualified to administer or supervise a specific treatment. Examples include:

- Prescribing of medication when the Responsible Clinician is not a doctor;

- Programmes of psychological treatment or assessment of which the Responsible Clinician has a basic understanding but no specific expertise.

Another professional can take responsibility for specific treatments or assessments but must ensure:

- The Responsible Clinician is kept informed about the treatment; and

- Decisions about the treatment are discussed with the Responsible Clinician and are consistent with the overall treatment plan and care pathway.

The person in charge of a particular treatment is expected to submit a report to a Tribunal or Manager's Hearing in addition to the Responsible Clinician's report.

Doctors approved under Section 12

Whilst the 2007 revision of the Act abandoned the 'doctor only' role of Responsible Medical Officer, it retains Section 12, which applies only to doctors.

Definition

A doctor who has been approved by the Secretary of State (or the Welsh Ministers) under the Act as having special experience in the diagnosis or treatment of mental disorder.

Only a doctor who is approved under Section 12:

- Can make certain medical recommendations; or

- Give certain medical evidence to courts under the Act.

Doctors who are Approved Clinicians:

- Are treated as though they are approved under Section 12 of the Act; so

- Training as an Approved Clinician has largely replaced training for approval under Section 12.

Nominated deputy

This is a doctor or Approved Clinician to whom the Responsible Clinician may delegate certain powers, including recommending detention under the holding power in Section 5 of the Act.

Approved Mental Health Professional (AMHP)

The 2007 revision abolished the role of Approved Social Worker (ASW) and replaced it with the role of Approved Mental Health Professional (AMHP).

Definition

An AMHP is a mental health professional approved by a local social services authority (LSSA) to carry out various functions under the Act.

The new role is similar to that of the ASW, with added responsibilities for SCT. It is open to four professions:

- Social worker;

- Mental health or learning disability nurse;

- Occupational therapist;

- Chartered psychologist.

A doctor cannot be an AMHP so the decision to restrict liberty is not a purely medical one. It is arguable, however, that allowing other health professionals to take on a role previously reserved for social workers has increased medical influence in a more general sense.

The AMHP is required to have:

- Professional training in mental health;
- Knowledge of local resources.

Functions of the AMHP include:

- To bring a social perspective to bear on decisions involving detention under the Act;
- To carry out assessments under the Act;
- To identify the Nearest Relative and to inform and consult as appropriate;
- To make an independent decision as to whether there are alternatives to detention under the Act;
- To make an application for detention under the Act or for Guardianship when the criteria are met and it is appropriate;
- To provide an outline report for the hospital when the patient is first admitted, giving reasons for admission and practical information;
- To provide a full report for the employer or LSSA on whose behalf they act when making an application;
- To assess a patient's suitability for SCT;
- To endorse when appropriate the Responsible Clinician's recommendation of SCT;
- To return to hospital detained or recalled SCT patients who are absent without leave (AWOL);
- To make an application to displace the Nearest Relative.

Guardian

A guardian is appointed:

- To help and supervise patients in the community;
- To oversee the patient's welfare; or
- To protect other people.

The Guardian may be:

- A local social services authority (LSSA); or
- A person approved by the LSSA (a private Guardian).

(See chapter 7 for discussion of the role of the Guardian.)

Hospital Manager(s)

Definition

The organisation or individual responsible for the operation of the Act in a particular hospital. Hospital Managers have the primary responsibility for seeing that the requirements of the Act are followed. They must ensure:

- Patients are detained only as the Act allows;
- Treatment accords with the provisions of the Act; and
- Patients are fully informed of their rights and supported in exercising them.

Ultimately, the Hospital Manager is an NHS Trust, an NHS Foundation Trust or the owner(s) of an independent hospital. In practice, the powers are delegated; most of the relevant decisions are taken by people they authorise to act on their behalf.

Although SCT patients are not in a hospital, the managers of the 'Responsible Hospital' have the same responsibilities.

Hospital Managers' power of discharge

Hospital Managers' functions under the Act include a power of discharge (except in the case of restricted patients), which is usually delegated to a Manager's panel of three or more people. Members are appointed specifically for the purpose and are not employees of the hospital concerned. (See chapter 6 for a discussion of Managers' Hearings.)

Duties in respect of victims of crime[1]

Hospital Managers have certain responsibilities in relation to unrestricted patients detained under Part 3 of the Act. They must make arrangements to:

- Advise victims if the patient's discharge is being considered, or if the patient is about to be discharged;

- Pass on representations from victims to those making decisions about discharge or SCT;

- Pass on to victims certain information received from the clinicians making decisions about discharge or SCT;

- Inform victims who wish to be told:

  - if the patient is to have SCT;

  - if there are any conditions relating to contact with the victim or the victim's family;

  - if there is any variation of such conditions;

  - and when the order is to end.

- Inform Responsible Clinicians of any representations made by the victim about the conditions attached to SCT.

Similar conditions attach to restricted patients but responsibility lies with the Probation Service rather than the Hospital Managers.

Other powers and duties

Hospital Managers must:

- Ensure valid authority for detention, including ensuring the paperwork is in order;

- Arrange for detained and SCT patients to be given information about the Act and their rights;

---

[1] Domestic Violence, Crime and Victims Act 2004.

- Refer a patient's case to the Tribunal in the circumstances set out in Section 68 of the Act;

- Ensure that patients aged under 18 years are accommodated in an environment suitable for their age, subject to their mental health treatment needs.[2]

They may:

- Discharge detained patients (see above);

- Authorise the transfer of detained patients from one hospital to another;

- Authorise the transfer of detained patients into Guardianship with the agreement of the relevant LSSA;

- Withhold outgoing post from detained patients if the addressee has made a written request (to them, to the Responsible Clinician or to the Secretary of State) that such post should be withheld.[3] The action must be recorded in writing and the patient informed.

Managers of high-security hospitals have wider powers under Section 134 to withhold incoming or outgoing mail. Their decisions in this respect:

- Should be supported by a written policy;

- Are subject to review by the Commission.

The Secretary of State for Health has issued directions requiring the managers of high-security hospitals to take similar action in relation to correspondence between patients, telephone calls and items brought in from outside the hospital.

Independent Mental Health Advocate (IMHA)

The 2007 revision of the Act created the role of IMHA. See chapter 5 for a fuller discussion of this role.

Definition

An IMHA is a specialised advocate trained to work within the framework

---

[2] Mental Health Act 1983 (2008) Section 131A.
[3] Mental Health Act 1983 (2008) Section 134.

of the Act to meet the needs of patients, in order to provide an additional safeguard for patients subject to the Act.

IMHAs work with other advocacy or support services – that is, they are not an alternative to those services.

Eligibility for IMHA services[4]

Eligibility for IMHA services is denoted by the term 'qualifying patient'. It is defined as follows:

- Patients detained under the Act (even if on leave of absence) except for those detained under Sections 4, 5, 135 or 136;
- Conditionally discharged restricted patients;
- Patients subject to Guardianship or SCT;
- Any patient being considered for treatment to which Section 57 applies;
- Any patient under 18 being considered for ECT (or other treatment to which Section 58A applies).

The role of the IMHA

IMHAs must help patients to obtain information about and understand:

- Their rights under the Act;
- The rights of other relevant people such as the Nearest Relative;
- The parts of the Act which apply to them, including any conditions or restrictions to which they are subject;
- Any medical treatment they are receiving or might receive, including the reasons for it;
- The legal authority for providing that treatment as well as the safeguards and other applicable requirements of the Act.

IMHAs help patients to exercise their rights and ensure they can participate in decisions made about their care and treatment. In order to achieve these goals they may:

---

[4] Mental Health Act 1983 (2008) Section 130C.

- Represent them;

- Speak on their behalf;

- Provide support in any appropriate way.

The involvement of an IMHA does not affect:

- A patient's right to seek advice from a lawyer;

- The Nearest Relative's right to seek advice from a lawyer;

- Entitlement to legal aid.

Duty to inform patients[5]

There is a duty to inform patients about the availability of IMHAs. Information must be given orally and in writing to ensure as far as is practicable that patients understand help is available and how they can obtain it.

The duty rests with different people depending on the status of the patient:

Detained and SCT patients	The Hospital Managers
Guardianship	The responsible social services authority
Conditionally discharged restricted patient	Responsible Clinician
Informal patient	The doctor or Approved Clinician who first discusses the relevant treatment with the patient

- The duty must be carried out as soon as possible after the patient has met the criteria specified above.

- Except for informal patients and those detained under Part 3, a copy of the written information must also be given to the patient's Nearest Relative, subject to the usual considerations about confidentiality.

- The information to the Nearest Relative should make clear that IMHA is a service for the patient and not for the Nearest Relative.

[5] Mental Health Act 1983 (2008) Section 130D.

Access to help from the IMHA

A qualifying patient:

- May request help at any time;

- May choose to end the help he or she is receiving at any time.

If it is thought the patient may benefit but is unable or unwilling to request help, a request to the IMHA may be made by:

- The patient's Nearest Relative;

- An Approved Mental Health Professional (AMHP);

- The patient's Responsible Clinician.

In these circumstances, the IMHA must comply with any reasonable request, but the patient is under no obligation to agree to be interviewed or to accept help from the IMHA.

IMHA access to patients and professionals

Patients should have access to a telephone on which they can contact the independent mental health advocacy service and talk to them in private.[6]

IMHAs should:

- Have access to wards and other living areas;

- Be able to see patients in private when appropriate;

- Be able to attend meetings between patients and professionals at the patient's invitation.

The IMHA has a right to meet the patient in private when instructed by:

- The patient;

- The Nearest Relative;

- An AMHP; or

- The Responsible Clinician.

The normal rules on confidentiality apply to conversations between

---

[6] Department of Health, *Code of Practice: Mental Health Act 1983* (2008) para: 20.21.

professionals and IMHAs even when the conversation is at the patient's request.

IMHA access to patients' records

With the patient's consent, the IMHA has a right to see any medical or social services records relating to the patient's detention, treatment or aftercare. If the patient lacks capacity to consent (or competence in the case of a child), the holder of the records must allow the IMHA access if it is appropriate (considering all the facts of the case), and if the records are relevant to the IMHA's work. The key consideration in relation to the appropriateness of disclosure will be whether it is justified in the best interests of the patient, in accordance with the MCA. Professionals should start from the general position that it is in the patient's best interests to have an advocate who is well informed.[7]

Deputy (aka Court-appointed Deputy)

Definition

A Deputy is a person appointed by the Court of Protection under Section 16 of the MCA to take specified decisions on behalf of a person who lacks capacity to take those decisions.

(See chapter 13 for discussion of the role of deputies.)

---

[7] Department of Health, *Code of Practice: Mental Health Act 1983* (2008) para: 20.31.

Chapter 5

Independent Mental Health Advocates and the Nearest Relative

Independent Mental Health Advocates

The Mental Health Act 1983 was amended by the 2007 Act to include a new statutory role, the 'Independent Mental Health Advocate' (IMHA). The introduction of IMHAs is widely regarded as a positive move, which will help to eliminate unlawful or unjustifiable discrimination through supporting patients to become more involved in the decisions made about their care and treatment and to ensure that patients' rights under the Mental Health Act 1983 are respected.

Advocacy has been available to support patients in many mental health services for some years. IMHAs do not replace any other advocacy and support services that are available to patients or other mental health service users, but are intended to operate in conjunction with those services.

Who is eligible to be provided with an IMHA?

A 'qualifying patient' is defined in Section 130C of the Mental Health Act 1983 and covers all those liable to detention under the Act except those detained via emergency short-term detentions – that is, Sections 4, 5(2), 5(4), 135 or 136. It includes patients covered by community treatment orders and those subject to Guardianship, conditional discharge and those transferred from prison to hospital.

In addition, an informal patient becomes a qualifying patient when:

- He or she discusses with a registered medical practitioner or approved clinician the possibility of being given a form of treatment to which Section 57 of the Act applies (psychosurgery, surgical implantation of hormones and other treatments specified in regulations); or

- He or she is under 18 and discusses with a registered medical practitioner or approved clinician the possibility of being given a form of treatment to which Section 58A applies (electro-convulsive therapy).

Informal patients remain eligible until the treatment is finished (or stopped), or it is decided that they will not be given the treatment for the time being.

Role of the IMHA

Section 130B of the Mental Health Act 1983 sets out the role of the IMHA, which is to assist the patient in obtaining information about and understanding:

- The provisions of the Mental Health Act 1983 under which he or she is detained or otherwise subject to that Act;

- Any conditions or restrictions to which he or she is subject;

- What medical treatment is given to him or her or is proposed;

- Why this is given or proposed;

- The authority under which the treatment is to be given;

- The requirements of the Act which apply in connection with the giving of treatment; and

- The patient's rights under the Act and the rights of his or her nearest relative. (In addition, the IMHA can help in exercising those rights.)

To assist in undertaking this role, the IMHA has the right to visit and interview a patient in private, to visit and interview the medical staff and (with patient consent) to see the patient's medical and social services records.

Who can be appointed as an IMHA?

According to the regulations, only persons employed by the commissioning authority or by a contracted IMHA service provider can act as an IMHA.[1] The regulations also explain that any person appointed as an IMHA must:

- Have appropriate training or experience or a combination of both;

- Be a person of integrity and good character;

- Be able to act independently of any person who requests an IMHA to visit and interview the patient; and

- Be able to act independently of any person who is professionally concerned with a patient's medical treatment.

In determining if a person is of integrity and good character, he or she must have undergone an enhanced Criminal Records Bureau check.

An IMHA should be able to act independently of any person who is professionally concerned with the patient's medical treatment and be able to act independently of any person who requests that person to visit or interview a patient.[2]

An advocate is not to be regarded as professionally concerned with a patient's medical treatment if their only involvement in that treatment is that they:

- Are currently representing the patient as an IMHA; or

- Have represented them as an IMHA in the past.[3]

---

[1] The Mental Health Act 1983 (Independent Mental Health Advocates) (England) Regulations 2008 SI 2008/3166, regulation 3(1) and 3(2).
[2] The Mental Health Act 1983 (Independent Mental Health Advocates) (England) Regulations 2008 SI 2008/3166 regulation 6(2)(C) and 6(2)(D).
[3] The Mental Health Act 1983 (Independent Mental Health Advocates) (England) Regulations 2008 SI 2008/3166 regulation 7.

The regulations set out who must check that an individual meets the appointment requirements before they may act as an IMHA.

1. In the case of persons directly employed by a commissioning authority to act as an IMHA, the commissioning authority must be satisfied that the individual meets the IMHA appointment requirements.

2. In the case of persons employed by an IMHA service provider, the commissioning authority should include a requirement in the agreement with the IMHA service provider, that the IMHA service provider must be satisfied that the individual meets the IMHA appointment requirements.

Who must provide the IMHA service?

The obligation to provide the IMHA service falls on the PCTs. They will commission IMHA services for qualifying patients, but the regulations permit them to commission jointly or delegate commissioning to other PCTs, or as part of partnership arrangements with local social services authorities.

The issue that may arise, particularly in the private sector, is whether the obligation falls on the PCT commissioning the patient's placement or the PCT for the area where the hospital is located. In broad terms, the PCT responsible for commissioning mental health care for a qualifying patient will also be responsible for ensuring that that patient has access to an IMHA.

The regulations direct that the commissioning body, in exercising their statutory functions must, as far as reasonably practicable, have regard to the diverse circumstances (including but not limited to the ethnic, cultural and demographic needs) of qualifying patients in respect of whom that commissioning body may exercise those functions.[4]

Who must provide information about the IMHA service?

Section 130D of the Mental Health Act 1983 places a duty on the 'Responsible Person' to provide verbal and written information about IMHA services to qualifying patients. The Responsible Person includes:

---

[4] The Mental Health Act 1983 (Independent Mental Health Advocates) (England) Regulations 2008 SI 2008/3166 regulation 3.

- Managers of the hospital (in relation to detained patients and those placed on Supervised Community Treatment);

- The Responsible Clinician (in relation to conditionally discharged patients and informal patients where treatment under Section 57 or 58A is being discussed);

- The local services social authority (in relation to Guardianship);

- The registered medical practitioner or Approved Clinician (in relation to informal patients and informal patients where treatment under Section 57 or 58A is being discussed).

The Responsible Person must inform the patient of his or her right to an IMHA. If the patient subsequently decides to access the service, he or she may request the Responsible Person to refer him or her to the IMHA service or choose to contact the IMHA service directly him/herself.

IMHA visits

Under Section 130B(5) of the Mental Health Act 1983, IMHAs are placed under a statutory duty to comply with any reasonable request to visit a qualifying patient when a referral is made by any of the following people:

- The patient's Nearest Relative;

- The patient's Responsible Clinician;

- An Approved Mental Health Professional acting on behalf of a local social services authority.

The *Code of Practice* advises that Approved Mental Health Professionals and Responsible Clinicians should consider requesting an IMHA to visit a qualifying patient if he or she thinks that the patient might benefit from an IMHA's visit but is unable or unlikely, for whatever reason, to request an IMHA's help him/herself.[5]

Under Section 130B (3) of the Mental Health Act 1983, when helping qualifying patients, IMHAs have the right to:

1. To see and interview a patient in private;

2. To meet and interview professionals involved with the patient's care.

---

[5] Department of Health, *Code of Practice: Mental Health Act 1983* (2008) para: 20.19.

These rights mean that, in practice, IMHAs should be able to:

- Have access to wards and units on which patients are resident;

- See patients in private unless the patient is under close observation or in seclusion, or clinical staff advise against it for reasons of the IMHA's or the patient's safety; and

- Attend relevant meetings with staff at the request of the patient.

Access to information

Under Section 130B of the Mental Health Act 1983, for the purpose of providing help to a qualifying patient, IMHAs may require the production of and inspect any records relating to a patient's detention or treatment in any hospital or registered establishment or to any after-care services provided for the patient under Section 117 of the Mental Health Act 1983. IMHAs may also require the production of and inspect any records of or held by, a local social services authority, which relate to a patient.

Under Section 130B of the Mental Health Act 1983, IMHAs may access records only for the purpose of providing help to a qualifying patient in their role as an IMHA, and where the following conditions are met:

- Where the patient consents and has capacity to make this decision, IMHAs have a right to see any clinical or other records relating to the patient's detention or treatment in any hospital, or relating to any aftercare services provided to the patient. IMHAs have a similar right to see any records relating to the patient held by a local social services authority.[6]

- Where the patient does not have the capacity (or in the case of a child, the competence) to consent to an IMHA having access to his/her records, the holder of the records must allow the IMHA access if he or she thinks that it is appropriate and that the records in question are relevant to the help to be provided by the IMHA.[7]

Anyone who refuses, without reasonable cause, to produce records that an IMHA has a right to inspect may be guilty of the offence of obstruction under Section 129 of the Mental Health Act 1983.

---

[6] Department of Health, *Code of Practice: Mental Health Act 1983* (2008) para: 20.25.
[7] Department of Health, *Code of Practice: Mental Health Act 1983* (2008) para: 20.26.

The relationship between IMHAs and legal representatives

IMHAs are not the same as legal representatives and are not expected to perform duties undertaken by solicitors, such as representation at Tribunal hearings. The *Code of Practice* states clearly that the involvement of an IMHA does not affect a patient's right (nor the right of their Nearest Relative) to seek advice from a lawyer. Nor does it affect any entitlement to legal aid.[8]

The Nearest Relative

Under the Mental Health Act 1983, the role of the 'Nearest Relative' represents an important safeguard for the rights of patients. The person who is identified as the Nearest Relative has extensive powers in relation to the decision to impose compulsion – including the right to be consulted about decisions to detain, the right to block compulsory admission for treatment and the right to direct the patient's discharge.

Who is the Nearest Relative?

Identifying a patient's Nearest Relative can be straightforward, but it can equally be one of the most complex tasks in the Mental Health Act 1983 and mistakes are common. The Nearest Relative is identified by reference to Section 26 of the Act, which sets out a hierarchical list of 'relatives' and includes a number of rules for identifying the Nearest Relative from this list. The list of relatives, in order of ranking, is:

1. The patient's husband, wife or civil partner;

2. A partner who has lived with the patient as if they were their husband, wife or civil partner for more than six months;

3. The eldest child;

4. The elder parent;

5. The eldest brother or sister;

6. The eldest grandparent;

---

[8] Department of Health, *Code of Practice: Mental Health Act 1983* (2008) para: 20.11.

7. The eldest grandchild;

8. The eldest uncle or aunt;

9. The eldest nephew or niece;

10. Any other person with whom the patient has ordinarily resided for five years or more.

The rules for identifying a Nearest Relative

The Nearest Relative is identified by starting at the top of the list and working down. So, for example, if the patient has a husband, wife or civil partner, that person will be the Nearest Relative. If there is no one in this first category, you go to the second; if there is no one on the second you go to the third, and so on.

If there is more than one person in a category, the eldest takes priority as Nearest Relative. For example, if the rules in Section 26 indicate that a parent is the patient's Nearest Relative and both parents are still alive, then it is the elder of the two who is the Nearest Relative. If Section 26 indicates that the Nearest Relative should be a brother or sister, it is the oldest brother or sister who is the Nearest Relative.

A relative of the whole blood (e.g. a full brother or sister) takes precedence over one of the half-blood (e.g. a half-brother or half-sister) within any category of relatives (regardless of age).

If the patient is living with or being cared for by any person on the list, this person is the Nearest Relative. For example, if the patient lives with an uncle or aunt, that person will be the Nearest Relative even if the patient has a mother or father. Similarly, if the patient lives with a younger brother or sister, that person will be the Nearest Relative even if the patient has an older brother or sister, or a parent.

If the patient resides in the UK, then the Nearest Relative must also reside in the UK. For example, if the rules in Section 26 indicate that the eldest brother should be Nearest Relative but he lives abroad, then he cannot be the Nearest Relative. If the patient does not reside in the UK, then the Nearest Relative can be someone who is, similarly, not resident in the UK.

A Nearest Relative must be aged 18 or over (unless they are the patient's husband, wife, civil partner or parent).

Rules for children

An unmarried father who does not have parental responsibility for his child is not a relative for the purposes of this section.

If the patient is under 18 and in the care of a local authority, by virtue of a care order under the Children Act 1989, then the local authority will be the Nearest Relative in preference to any person except a husband, wife or civil partner.

If a 'Children's Guardian' (or 'Special Guardian') has been appointed for a child or young person under 18, that person (or all of them if there are more than one) will normally be deemed to be the Nearest Relative.

If a patient is under 18 and living with someone under a residence order, as defined under Section 8 of the Children Act 1989, then that person will normally be the Nearest Relative.

What happens if there is no Nearest Relative?

If no one qualifies as a Nearest Relative under the rules in Section 26, the County Court can appoint someone to act as Nearest Relative (see below).

Which patients do not have a Nearest Relative?

Restricted patients (including conditionally discharged patients) do not have a nearest relative for the purposes of the Act. Nor do patients remanded to hospital under Section 35 or 36, nor patients subject to interim hospital orders under Section 38.

Changing the Nearest Relative

The identity of the Nearest Relative can easily change due to new circumstances. For example, if the Nearest Relative dies, or a marriage or civil partnership ends (in cases where Nearest Relative is a spouse or civil partner), or the patient or another relative reaches 18, or the patient marries, and so on.

The Mental Health Act 1983 allows the Nearest Relative to be changed in certain circumstances. There are two ways that this can be done. The Nearest Relative can delegate their powers to someone else, or an application can be made to the County Court to displace the Nearest Relative and appoint someone else.

The Nearest Relative's power to delegate

The Nearest Relative may delegate his or her functions to any person (other than the patient or a person disqualified under Section 26(5)) who is willing to take on this role.

In the case of unrestricted Part 3 patients, the Nearest Relative cannot delegate his or her right to apply to the Tribunal on the patient's behalf.

Nearest Relatives may delegate their functions at any time, whether or not a question of admission to hospital or Guardianship has already arisen. The actual Nearest Relative may revoke the delegation at any time and thereby take back his/her rights.

Displacement

Upon receiving an application under Section 29 of the Act, the County Court may make an order directing that the functions of the Nearest Relative shall be exercised by another person or by a local authority. An application to the court can be made by:

1. The patient;

2. The patient's relative (not necessarily the Nearest Relative);

3. Any other person with whom the patient ordinarily resides; or

4. An Approved Mental Health Professional.

An application can rely only upon the grounds set out under Section 29(3), which are:

1. The patient has no Nearest Relative, or it cannot reasonably be determined whether the patient has any Nearest Relative, or who they are; or

2. The existing Nearest Relative is incapable of acting as Nearest Relative due to mental disorder of other illness; or

3. The existing Nearest Relative unreasonably objects to the application for the patient to be admitted for treatment or to be placed under Guardianship; or

4. The existing Nearest Relative has exercised his/her power to discharge the patient or is likely to exercise the rights in such a way as does not give due regard to the patient's welfare or to the interests of the public; or

> 5. The existing nearest relative is not a suitable person to act as such.

Under Section 29 of the Mental Health Act 1983, the County Court can order that the functions of the Nearest Relative shall be exercised by someone *else* regarded as suitable to act as such and who is willing to do so. There is no requirement that the person applying for displacement should have been living with the patient for any minimum period. The application may (but does not have to) nominate a person whom the applicant would like to be appointed as the acting Nearest Relative. Case law has established that the court may make an interim order appointing an acting Nearest Relative, pending its final decision.[9]

A Nearest Relative who is supplanted by virtue of an order made under Section 29 has a right to apply to a Tribunal for the patient's case to be reviewed. The application may be made within 12 months of the date of the County Court order and in any subsequent period of 12 months.[10]

Powers of the Nearest Relative

The person identified as the patient's Nearest Relative has a number of important rights and functions under the Mental Health Act 1983. These are discussed below.

The right to require an assessment to be made (Section 13(4))

The Nearest Relative can require the local authority to ask an Approved Mental Health Professional to consider the case with a view to admitting the patient to hospital.

If the person is not admitted to hospital, the Nearest Relative is entitled to a written explanation by the Approved Mental Health Professional of why an application was not made.

The right to apply for compulsory admission or Guardianship

The Nearest Relative can apply for admission to hospital under Sections 2, 3 and 4 and for Guardianship under Section 7. In practice, this rarely happens and the *Code of Practice* states clearly that the Approved Mental

---

[9] *R. v Uxbridge County Court, ex p. Binns* [2000] MHLR 179.
[10] Section 66(1)(h), Section 66(2)(g).

Health Professional should in the majority of cases be the preferred applicant since they are better placed to carry out this task.

Right to be consulted (Section 11(4))

Section 11(4) states that before making an application for detention under Section 3 or Guardianship, Approved Mental Health Professionals must consult the Nearest Relative, unless it is not reasonably practicable or would involve unreasonable delay.

The right to object to Section 3 admission or Guardianship (Section 11(4))

An application for admission to hospital under Section 3 or for Guardianship can proceed only if the Approved Mental Health Professional has taken reasonable steps to consult the Nearest Relative and obtain his or her agreement to admission. If the Nearest Relative objects, an application under Section 3 or Guardianship can be made only if the Nearest Relative is displaced by the County Court (see above) and the new Nearest Relative does not object.

The right to order discharge of the patient (Section 23)

If the Nearest Relative wants the patient to be discharged from detention in hospital (under Section 2 or 3), Guardianship or Supervised Community Treatment, he or she must give the Hospital Managers at least 72 hours' notice in writing. In the case of detention in hospital or Supervised Community Treatment, the patient must then be discharged within 72 hours of receipt of the letter, unless the Responsible Clinician certifies that in his or her opinion the patient is likely to present a danger to him/herself or to others.

If the patient is detained under Section 2 of the Mental Health Act, there is nothing more the Nearest Relative can do after the Responsible Clinician has overruled the request for discharge. If the patient is detained under Section 3 or is under Supervised Community Treatment, however, the Nearest Relative can apply to the Tribunal.

The Responsible Clinician has no power to prevent the Nearest Relative obtaining discharge of a patient from Guardianship.

Rights to information

Under Section 11(3) of the Act, the Approved Mental Health Professional must take such steps as are practicable to inform the patient's Nearest Relative that an application for admission to hospital under Section 2 is to be or has been made and of his or her power to discharge the patient. This information can be given orally or in writing.

Unless a patient objects, Section 132(4) of the Mental Health Act requires Hospital Managers to take such steps as are practicable to ensure the Nearest Relative is given a copy of any information given to the detained patient or patient subject to Supervised Community Treatment. The managers must inform the Nearest Relative about, amongst other things, the right to apply to the Tribunal.

The Nearest Relative should be given seven days' notice of a relative's discharge, unless the patient objects (Section 133).

The process of consulting Nearest Relatives

The *Code of Practice* suggests that, when consulting a Nearest Relative for the purposes of the Mental Health Act, Approved Mental Health Professionals, should where possible:

- Ascertain the Nearest Relative's views about both the patient's needs and the Nearest Relative's own needs in relation to the patient;

- Inform the Nearest Relative of the reasons for considering an application for detention and what the effects of such an application would be; and

- Inform the Nearest Relative of his/her role and rights under the Act.[11]

Circumstances in which the Nearest Relative need not be informed or consulted

According to the *Code of Practice*, the circumstances where a Nearest Relative may not need to be consulted or informed include:

- It is not practicable for the Approved Mental Health Professional to obtain sufficient information to establish the identity or location of the Nearest Relative, or where to do so would require

---

[11] Department of Health, *Code of Practice: Mental Health Act 1983* (2008) para: 4.64.

an excessive amount of investigation involving unreasonable delay; and

- Consultation is not possible because of the Nearest Relative's own health or mental incapacity.[12]

The *Code* also provides advice on circumstances where the Nearest Relative should not be consulted or informed because doing so would have a detrimental impact on the patient, which would result in infringement of the patient's right to respect for his/her privacy and family life under Article 8 of the European Convention on Human Rights. This includes cases where patients are likely to suffer emotional distress, deterioration in their mental health, physical harm, or financial or other exploitation as a result of the consultation.[13]

If they do not consult or inform the Nearest Relative, Approved Mental Health Professionals should record their reasons.[14] The *Code* also states that consultation must not be avoided purely because it is thought that the Nearest Relative might object to the application.[15]

The *Code of Practice* suggests that, when consulting a Nearest Relative for the purposes of the Mental Health Act, Approved Mental Health Professionals should where possible:

1. Ascertain the Nearest Relative's views about both the patient's needs and the Nearest Relative's own needs in relation to the patient;

2. Inform the Nearest Relative of the reasons for considering an application for detention and what the effects of such an application would be; and

3. Inform the Nearest Relative of his/her role and rights under the Act.

---

[12] Department of Health, *Code of Practice: Mental Health Act 1983* (2008) para: 4.59.
[13] Department of Health, *Code of Practice: Mental Health Act 1983* (2008) para: 4.60.
[14] Department of Health, *Code of Practice: Mental Health Act 1983* (2008) para: 4.63.
[15] Department of Health, *Code of Practice: Mental Health Act 1983* (2008) para: 4.63.

Chapter 6

The Tribunal and Hospital Managers' Hearings

The Tribunal

In England, the First-tier Tribunal (Mental Health) hears applications and references for patients under the powers of the Mental Health Act 1983. Specifically, it has the power to decide whether patients should continue to be detained under the Act or continue to remain subject to Supervised Community Treatment (SCT), Guardianship or conditional discharge, as applicable. There is a separate Mental Health Tribunal for Wales. There is also an Upper Tribunal, which can hear appeals of decisions made by the First-tier Tribunal on a point of law.

Tribunals for mental health patients were first introduced by the Mental Health Act 1959 and were known as Mental Health Review Tribunals. The Mental Health Act 1983 extended the powers of Mental Health Review Tribunals, giving all detained patients a right to have their continued detention in hospital reviewed. The First-tier and Upper Tribunal replaced Mental Health Review Tribunals as a result of the Tribunals, Courts and Enforcement Act 2007. In practice, however, the jurisdiction of the First-tier Tribunal (Mental Health) is exactly the same as that of the Mental Health Review Tribunal.

Powers of the Tribunal

Powers of discharge

The Tribunal is an independent judicial body that operates under the provisions of the Mental Health Act 1983. Its main purpose is to review the cases of patients detained under the Mental Health Act 1983 and to direct the discharge of any patients where the statutory criteria for detention set out in Section 72 have not been satisfied (see below). In some cases, the Tribunal also has the discretion to discharge patients even though the legal grounds for detention still exist (although in practice this power is used rarely). This does not apply to restricted patients. The Tribunal has no general discretion to discharge restricted patients. It may discharge them only where it is required by the Act to do so (see below).

The Tribunal also reviews the cases of people subject to SCT, conditional discharge and Guardianship. The Tribunal, therefore, provides a significant safeguard for patients who are subject to the powers of the Mental Health Act 1983.

When discharging patients from detention (but not SCT or Guardianship), the Tribunal may direct that the discharge will take effect at a specified future date. This is commonly known as 'deferred discharge'. Otherwise, discharges by the Tribunal *take effect immediately*.

Power to make recommendations

If the Tribunal decides not to discharge a patient from detention, it may recommend that the patient be granted leave of absence or be transferred to another hospital, with a view to facilitating the patient's discharge on a future occasion.

The Tribunal cannot discharge patients onto SCT, and is not required to discharge patients absolutely from detention just because it thinks that SCT might be appropriate for them. However, the Tribunal may recommend that the Responsible Clinician considers whether to discharge a patient onto SCT.

The Tribunal's recommendations are not binding on Hospital Managers or Responsible Clinicians (although they must be considered). If its recommendations are not put into practice, the Tribunal may (if it wishes) further consider a patient's case, without the patient or anyone else having to make a new application.

Statutory criteria for detention and discharge

Section 72 of the Mental Health Act 1983 directs Tribunals to discharge patients from hospital, Guardianship or SCT if specified criteria are not satisfied.

Section 2 patients

In the case of a Section 2 patient, the Tribunal must direct the discharge of the patient if they are not satisfied:

1. That he or she is suffering from a mental disorder or from a mental disorder of a nature or degree which warrants his/her detention in a hospital for assessment (or for assessment followed by medical treatment) for at least a limited period; or

2. That his or her detention is justified in the interests of his or her own health or safety or with a view to the protection of other persons.

Other detained patients

The Tribunal must direct the discharge of other detained patients (except restricted patients) if they are not satisfied:

1. That he or she is suffering from a mental disorder of a nature or degree which makes it appropriate for him/her to receive medical treatment; or

2. That it is necessary for the health or safety of the patient or for the protection of other persons that he or she should receive such treatment; or

3. That appropriate treatment is available; or

4. In the case of an application by a Nearest Relative to the Tribunal where the Responsible Clinician has barred the Nearest Relative's discharge powers, that the patient, if released, would be likely to act in a manner dangerous to other persons or to him/herself.

Community patients

The Tribunal must direct the discharge of community patients (i.e. those subject to Supervised Community Treatment) if they are not satisfied:

1. That he or she is suffering from a mental disorder of a nature or degree which makes it appropriate for him or her to receive medical treatment; or

2. That it is necessary for the health or safety of the patient or for the protection of other persons that he or she should receive such treatment; or

3. That it is necessary that the Responsible Clinician should be able to exercise the power under Section 17(E)(1) of the Mental Health Act 1983 to recall the patient to hospital; or

4. That appropriate treatment is available; or

5. In the case of an application by a Nearest Relative to the Tribunal where the Responsible Clinician has barred the Nearest Relative's discharge powers, that the patient, if released, would be likely to act in a manner dangerous to other persons or to him/herself.

Guardianship

The Tribunal may in any case discharge a patient subject to Guardianship and must discharge that patient where:

1. He or she is not suffering from a mental disorder; or

2. It is not necessary in the interests of the welfare of the patient or for the protection of other persons that the patient should remain under Guardianship.

Restricted patients

The Tribunal must discharge patients who are subject to a restriction order (other than patients who have been conditionally discharged and not recalled to hospital) if it is not satisfied that the criteria for continued detention for treatment under a hospital order are met. The criteria are as follows:

1. He or she is suffering from a mental disorder of a nature or degree which makes it appropriate for him or her to receive

medical treatment; or

2. It is necessary for the health or safety of the patient or for the protection of other persons that he or she should receive such treatment; or

3. Appropriate treatment is available.

The discharge must be conditional, unless the Tribunal is satisfied that it is not appropriate for the patient to remain liable to be recalled to hospital for further treatment (i.e. to be made subject to conditional discharge).

If the patient is to be discharged absolutely, the discharge takes effect immediately and the patient stops being subject to both the restriction order and the accompanying hospital order. The Tribunal cannot defer an absolute discharge.

Where the Tribunal is required to discharge a restricted patient conditionally, it may (but does not have to) impose conditions with which the patient is to comply. The Secretary of State for Justice may also impose conditions and vary those imposed by the Tribunal.

As with other restricted patients, the Tribunal has no general discretion to discharge patients subject to hospital and limitation directions or restricted transfer directions.

In addition, because these patients are liable to resume serving their sentence of imprisonment (or its equivalent) if they no longer require treatment in hospital, special arrangements apply where the Tribunal believes that the criteria for discharge from detention are met.

What cannot be considered by the Tribunal

The Tribunal does not deal with the discharge of patients who are:

- Detained under the emergency power in Section 4;

- Detained under the 'holding powers' in Section 5;

- Remanded to hospital under Sections 35 or 36;

- Subject to an interim hospital order under Section 38;

- Detained in a place of safety under Sections 135 or 136; or

- Voluntary patients under Section 131 of the Mental Health Act.

The Tribunal has jurisdiction only within the Mental Health Act 1983 and, therefore, it cannot consider cases:

- Where a hospital patient is being deprived of liberty under the Mental Capacity Act 2005 (see chapter 14); or

- Where it is believed that the detention is unlawful (in which case the patient is entitled to apply for judicial review and/or habeas corpus).

Although the Tribunal reviews the cases of patients detained in hospital under the Mental Health Act 1983, it cannot actually decide whether or not the decision to make a person subject to those legal powers was wrong in the first place. Nor can it assess or pass judgement on whether the patient is receiving appropriate treatment or care. It decides whether, at the time of the hearing, the patient concerned should remain subject to the relevant aspect of the Act.

Informing patients of their right to apply to a Tribunal

Under Section 132 of the Mental Health Act 1983, Hospital Managers are under a duty to take steps to ensure that patients understand their rights to apply for a Tribunal hearing. All information must be given orally and in writing. Unless the patient objects, the information is normally also given to the Nearest Relative.

The *Code of Practice* also advises that Hospital Managers and the local social services authority should advise patients of their entitlement to free legal advice and representation and they should do so whenever:

- Patients are first detained in hospital, received into Guardianship or discharged to SCT;

- Their detention or Guardianship is renewed or SCT is extended; and

- Their status under the Mental Health Act 1983 changes – for example, if they move from detention under Section 2 to detention under Section 3 or if their community treatment order is revoked.

When can a patient apply to the Tribunal for a hearing?

An application to a Tribunal has to be made within a certain time period, and only one application per period is allowed. The basic rules can be summarised as follows:

- Patients detained under Section 2 must make an appeal within 14 days of the start of their detention. If, between making the appeal and the hearing, the patient is placed on Section 3, the Tribunal will still hearing the original appeal and it will not affect the patient's right to appeal under Section 3.

- Patients detained under Section 3 can only appeal to the Tribunal once in any six-month period.

- Patients detained under Section 37 can apply to the Tribunal only after the initial six months' period has elapsed. Thereafter, their rights of appeal are the same as for Section 3 patients.

Time limits for hearings

For patients detained under Section 2, the hearing must take place within seven days of receipt of the application by the Tribunal administrators.

For patients detained under Section 3 and other non-restricted patients, the hearing will normally take place within eight weeks.

For restricted patients, the hearing will normally take place within 16 weeks.

Making an application

The patient, his or her legal representative or the Nearest Relative may complete an application form for a Tribunal hearing.

Applications can be withdrawn only in writing and normally should include a letter from the patient's solicitor. The Tribunal or the Regional Tribunal Judge will then decide whether to accept the withdrawal.

Automatic reviews

Most patients detained under the Mental Health Act 1983 can apply to the Tribunal to be discharged. In practice, many patients never apply and it is for this reason the safeguard of automatic periodic reviews was introduced. Automatic reviews apply in a number of cases. These include:

- Patients detained under Section 3 who have not had their detention reviewed by the Tribunal within the last six months; and

- Patients who have had their detention renewed and have not appealed to the Tribunal in the last three years (if aged 18 years or over) or the last one year (if aged less than 18 years).

Also, the Secretary of State may at any time refer to the Tribunal the case of any patient detained under Part 2 of the Mental Health Act 1983.

Members of the Tribunal

Each Tribunal panel must consist of three members: a legal member, who is the judge, a medical specialist and a third member from a non-medical or non-legal background. Regional Tribunal Judges determine which members should sit at a particular hearing.

The role of the legal member

The role of the legal member is to chair the Tribunal hearing. He or she is responsible for making sure that the proceedings are conducted fairly, that the legal requirements of the Mental Health Act 1983 are properly observed and advising on any questions of law which may arise. The legal member is also responsible, in consultation with other members of the Tribunal, for drafting the reasons for the decision, and for signing the record of the decision. Legal members are appointed by the Lord Chancellor and are required to have 'such legal experience, as the Lord Chancellor considers suitable'.

The role of the medical member

The medical member of the Tribunal is required to carry out an examination of the patient before the hearing and to take any steps that he or she considers necessary to form an opinion of the patient's mental condition. He or she will be able to advise the other members of the Tribunal on any medical matters. If his/her opinion differs significantly from other medical witnesses, then this should be made known at the beginning of the hearing. This is because it would be unfair and contrary to a basic principle of natural justice if the Tribunal members were to take notice of information that had not been shared with all the other parties at the hearing. The medical member is normally a consultant psychiatrist of several years' standing.

The role of the third member

The third member (sometimes known as the 'lay member') is intended to provide balance to the Tribunal as a representative of the community outside the legal and medical professions. He or she will normally have a background of working in the health and welfare fields in the NHS, voluntary organisations or private health sector.

The role of the Regional Tribunal Judges

There are two Regional Tribunal Judges who are responsible for:

- Appointing members to particular hearings;
- Making judicial decisions and giving directions;
- Organising training for members; and
- Handling complaints about a member's conduct.

Who can attend a Tribunal hearing?

There are a number of people who can attend a hearing, including a solicitor, members of the clinical team working with the patient and individuals from the patient's family. The patient may or may not attend, depending on the circumstances. If the patient decides not to attend, the Tribunal can still decide to proceed with the hearing.

The *Code of Practice* points out that it is important that the patient's Responsible Clinician attends the Tribunal, supported by other staff involved in the patient's care where appropriate, as his/her evidence is crucial for making the case for the patient's continued detention or SCT under the Act. If the Responsible Clinician cannot attend, then the Tribunal will normally expect to see a deputy who, in the opinion of the Responsible Clinician, has sufficient knowledge and experience of the patient.

Which professionals will attend a hearing will depend on the circumstances of the individual case. They may include one or more of the following:

- The professionals who have prepared reports for the hearing;

- A nurse who knows the patient well;

- A member of the community mental health team;

- An Approved Mental Health Professional;

- A social services representative (particularly in cases where the patient may be eligible for Section 117);

- The patient's Independent Mental Health Act Advocate.

Legal representation

Patients are entitled to be represented at Tribunal hearings. The Law Society provides an approved list of solicitors who are accredited to represent patients at Tribunals on its website. Patients are equally entitled not to have a legal representative, or to represent themselves.

Legal aid is available through the Community Legal Service Fund to fund legal advice and representation before the Tribunal without requiring any assessment of the patient's means. Legal aid for appeals to the Upper Tribunal is means-tested and subject to a merits test.

The hearing

Tribunals are not as formal as court proceedings, but are none the less likely to be a difficult experience for a patient. Patients are entitled to have someone to represent them and may also bring along a family member or a friend for support. It is the role of the legal member and other members of the Tribunal to ensure that the patient has the opportunity to communicate his or her views, either personally or through a representative.

Tribunal hearings are normally in private unless the patient requests a public hearing and the Tribunal accepts the request. For detained patients, the hearing will usually take place in the hospital where the patient is detained. The Tribunal will seek to avoid formality to help put the patient at ease. Normally, the patient will be present throughout the hearing, unless one of the parties requests otherwise. The Tribunal must agree to such a request. The patient's representative will, however, be entitled to be present throughout the hearing.

As the *Code of Practice* notes, it is for those who believe that a patient should continue to be detained or remain on SCT to prove their case, not for the patient to disprove it. They will therefore need to present the Tribunal with sufficient evidence to support continuing liability to detention or SCT. This evidence is normally based on clinical and social reports.

The *Code of Practice* advises that a Responsible Clinician can attend the hearing solely as a witness or as the nominated representative of the Responsible Authority. As a representative of the Responsible Authority, the Responsible Clinician has the ability to call and cross-examine witnesses and to make submissions to the Tribunal. However, this may not always be desirable where it is envisaged that the Responsible Clinician will have to continue working closely with a patient.

A Tribunal has the power to obtain any information it thinks necessary, including the power to subpoena witnesses.

When does the Tribunal make its decision?

The Tribunal normally makes its decision at the end of the hearing and will relay this to the patient or their representative at that time. This will be followed up with written reasons a few days later.

If the Tribunal makes statutory recommendations – for example, for transfer to another hospital or for leave of absence – the hospital is not legally obliged to follow them but the Tribunal can reconvene at a later stage to find out why their recommendations have not been followed, and rehear the matter as appropriate.

Adjournments

The Tribunal has the power to adjourn a hearing. This may be for further information in the form of reports or for a witness to attend a reconvened hearing. Directions may be made as to when and how the information should be provided, and for the issuing of a subpoena if necessary. A Tribunal cannot adjourn to monitor a patient's progress.

Upper Tribunal

The Upper Tribunal is also established under the Tribunals, Courts and Enforcement Act 2007. Its role is to determine appeals against decisions of the First-tier Tribunal. It also hears appeals against decisions of the Tribunal for Wales.

Appeals to the Upper Tribunal may be made only on a point of law, and only with the permission of the First-tier Tribunal or the Upper Tribunal itself. Before deciding whether to grant permission to appeal, the First-tier Tribunal will first consider whether to review its own decision.

If it upholds an appeal, the Upper Tribunal may make a new decision itself, or it may remit the case back to the First-tier Tribunal to be heard again.

Administrative Justice and Tribunals Council

The working and constitution of the First-tier Tribunal and the Upper Tribunal are subject to the oversight of the Administrative Justice and Tribunals Council.

Managers' Hearings

The Hospital Managers are non-executive directors of the hospital's Board of Directors. They act on behalf of the NHS Trust that runs the hospital.

Section 23 of the Mental Health Act 1983 gives Hospital Managers the power to discharge most detained patients and all patients on SCT. They may not discharge patients remanded to hospital under Sections 35 or 36 of the Act or who are subject to interim hospital orders under Section 38. They also cannot discharge restricted patients without the consent of the Secretary of State for Justice.

The Managers can also hold hearings at their own discretion. In practice, Managers' Hearings will be held:

- At the patient's request (unless there has been a recent Managers' Hearing and the Managers are satisfied that the circumstances considered then are unchanged in all important respects);
- On the renewal of detention;

- When the Nearest Relative is barred from discharging the patient.

Hospital Managers must undertake a review if the patient's Responsible Clinician submits to them a report under Section 20 of the Act renewing detention or under Section 20A extending SCT.

The Act does not define specific criteria that the Hospital Managers must use when considering discharge. The *Code of Practice*, however, states that the Managers must consider whether the grounds for continued detention or continued SCT under the Act are satisfied and sets out a series of questions for Managers' Panels to consider, to ensure that this is done in a systematic and consistent way.

The Mental Health Act 1983 does not define the procedure for reviewing a patient's detention or SCT. The *Code of Practice* recommends that Managers' Panels should:

- Adopt and apply a procedure which is fair and reasonable;

- Not make irrational decisions – that is, decisions which no Managers' Panel, properly directing itself as to the law and on the available information, could have made; and

- Not act unlawfully – that is, contrary to the provisions of the Act and any other legislation (including the Human Rights Act 1998 and relevant equality and anti-discrimination legislation).

Chapter 7

Care and Treatment in the Community

Supervised Community Treatment,
Guardianship and Section 17 leave of absence

The Mental Health Act 1983 is not limited to the care and treatment of people detained in hospital. It also sets out a number of powers that can be used when people have left hospital and are living in the community. This chapter focuses on the three community orders: Supervised Community Treatment (SCT), which was added to the 1983 Act by the Mental Health Act 2007; Guardianship; and Section 17 leave of absence.

There are two further community orders provided under the Mental Health Act, both of which apply to mentally disordered offenders. These are (1) Section 37 Guardianship and (2) conditional discharge, which applies to patients who are subject to a restriction order, who have been conditionally discharged from hospital. Both of these provisions are covered in more detail in Chapter 10.

Supervised Community Treatment (SCT)

SCT allows patients to be discharged from hospital to live in the community, whilst still subject to powers under the 1983 Act and liable to recall to hospital for treatment if this is necessary. According to the *Code of Practice* the aim of SCT is to 'allow patients to be safely treated in the community rather than under detention in hospital, and to provide a way to help prevent relapse and any harm – to the patient or to others – that this might cause'.[1]

SCT was added to the 1983 Act in 2008, following the implementation of the Mental Health Act 2007, and has replaced 'supervised aftercare'.[2] It is carried out through the mechanism of Community Treatment Orders (CTO). Patients who are subject to a CTO are referred to in the legislation as 'community patients'.

Who can make a CTO?

The decision to make a CTO is taken by the Responsible Clinician, with the agreement of an Approved Mental Health Professional, who must state in writing that he or she agrees that the relevant criteria are satisfied (see below) and that it is appropriate to make the order. According to the *Code of Practice*, consultation at an early stage with the patient and those involved in the patient's care will be important.[3]

The Tribunal can recommend that SCT should be considered, where it decides not to discharge a patient. It will then be up to the Responsible Clinician to carry out an assessment to decide if SCT is appropriate for the patient.

Eligibility for SCT

To be eligible to be considered for SCT, the patient must be detained for treatment under Section 3 of the Mental Health Act or under an unrestricted Part 3 order – such as:

- A hospital order (unrestricted) made under Sections 37 or 51(5);

- A transfer direction (unrestricted) made under Sections 47 or 48;

- A hospital direction under Section 45A where the limitation direction has ceased to have effect.

---

[1] Department of Health, *Code of Practice: Mental Health Act 1983* (2008) para: 25.2.
[2] Supervised aftercare was set out in Sections 25A to 25J of the 1983 Act which had been inserted by the Mental Health (Patients in the Community) Act 1995.
[3] Department of Health, *Code of Practice: Mental Health Act 1983* (2008) para: 25.6.

Criteria

The relevant criteria that must be met are that:

- The patient is suffering from a mental disorder of a nature or degree which makes it appropriate for him/her to receive medical treatment;

- It is necessary for his/her health or safety or for the protection of other persons, that he/she should receive such treatment;

- Subject to the patient being liable to be recalled, such treatment can be provided without him/her continuing to be detained in a hospital;

- It is necessary that the responsible clinician should be able to exercise the power under Section 17E(1) to recall the patient to hospital; and

- Appropriate medical treatment is available for the patient.

In determining whether these criteria are met, the Responsible Clinician must have regard to:

- The patient's history of mental disorder and any other relevant factors; and

- What risk there would be of a deterioration in the patient's condition if he/she were not detained in a hospital (as a result, for example, of his/her refusing or neglecting to receive the medical treatment he/she requires for his/her mental disorder).

Conditions

The CTO must specify conditions with which the community patient is required to comply while the order remains in force. In all cases, the patients are required to make themselves available for medical examination – in particular, for the purposes of renewal of the CTO and a Part 4A certificate.

The Responsible Clinician, with the agreement of the Approved Mental Health Professional (AMHP), can also set further conditions that are necessary or appropriate to:

- Ensure the patient receives medical treatment;

- Prevent a risk of harm to the patient's health or safety; or

- Protect other people.

Examples of such conditions might include:

- When and where the patient is to receive treatment in the community;

- Where the patient is to live; and

- Avoidance of known risk factors or high-risk situations relevant to the patient's mental disorder.[4]

According to the *Code of Practice* the conditions should:

- Be kept to a minimum number consistent with achieving their purpose;

- Restrict the patient's liberty as little as possible while being consistent with achieving their purpose;

- Have a clear rationale, linked to one or more of the purposes set out above; and

- Be clearly and precisely expressed, so that the patient can readily understand what is expected.

Enforcing the conditions

If a community patient fails to comply with either of the mandatory conditions – (1) to make themselves available for medical examination for the purposes of renewing the CTO or (2) to allow the completion of a Part 4A certificate – then the Responsible Clinician can recall the patient to hospital.

The other conditions attached to a CTO are not in themselves enforceable, but if a patient fails to comply with one of them, then that fact may be taken into account when deciding whether or not to recall the patient back into hospital. However, a patient cannot be recalled unless the criteria for recall in Section 17E are met (see below). The Act makes it clear that if the criteria for recall are met, the recall power may still be exercised even if the patient is complying with the conditions.

---

[4] Department of Health, *Code of Practice: Mental Health Act 1983* (2008) para: 25.34.

The *Code of Practice* advises that if a patient is not complying with any condition of the CTO, then the reasons for this need to be properly investigated. It also advises that options including recall to hospital, varying the conditions and changing the patient's care plan should be considered.[5]

Varying and suspending conditions

The Responsible Clinician has the power to vary or suspend the conditions attached to a CTO. There is no requirement to obtain an Approved Mental Health Professional's agreement before so doing, but the *Code of Practice* suggests that it would be good practice to discuss varying the conditions where the conditions had recently been agreed, with the same Approved Mental Health Professional who agreed to them.

Duration and renewal

A CTO will initially apply for six months and can subsequently be extended for a further six months, then for further periods of one year at a time. Before the CTO can be extended, the Responsible Clinician must examine the patient in the two months preceding the expiry date – and must consult at least one other person who has been professionally concerned with the patient's medical treatment. An Approved Mental Health Professional must also state in writing that he or she agrees that the relevant criteria are satisfied and it is appropriate to make the order.

The grounds for determining whether to extend the CTO are the same as those that are applied to determine whether it is appropriate to make a patient subject to a CTO (see above).

Recall to hospital

Criteria for recall

The Responsible Clinician may recall a patient on a CTO to hospital if:

- The patient needs to receive treatment in hospital for his or her mental disorder; and

- There would be a risk of harm to the health or safety of the patient or to other persons if the patient were not recalled.

---

[5] Department of Health, *Code of Practice: Mental Health Act 1983* (2008) para: 25.40.

The Responsible Clinician can recall the community patient to hospital if the patient fails to comply with either of the mandatory conditions: (1) to make him/herself available for medical examination for the purposes of renewing the CTO or (2) to allow the completion of a Part 4A certificate. The *Code of Practice* advises that before recalling a community patient for this reason, the Responsible Clinician should consider whether he/she has a valid reason for not complying and should take any further action accordingly.[6]

The Code also advises that recall to hospital for treatment should not become a regular or normal event for any patient on SCT.[7]

Procedures for recall
The power of recall is exercised by the Responsible Clinician giving notice in writing to the patient – and once this notice has been served, the Hospital Managers are given the authority to re-detain the patient.

Following the decision to recall the patient by the Responsible Clinician, the patient can be taken and conveyed to hospital by any Approved Mental Health Professional, officer on the staff of the hospital, any constable or by any person authorised in writing by the Responsible Clinician or the Hospital Managers.

If necessary, a warrant under Section 135(2) of the 1983 Act may be obtained from a magistrate's court to allow the police to enter the patient's premises and recall the patient, by force if necessary. The police can be accompanied by a doctor or any other person authorised to recall the patient, such as an Approved Mental Health Professional.

Effect of recall
The Act allows the patient to be detained on recall for up to 72 hours before the CTO must be revoked or the patient is discharged back into the community. During this period the patient can be treated without consent, subject to safeguards under Part 4 and Part 4A of the Act.

The Responsible Clinician can treat and release the patient at any point in the 72-hour period, following which the patient will remain subject to the CTO and will be required to continue complying with the conditions imposed.

---

[6] Department of Health, *Code of Practice: Mental Health Act 1983* (2008) para: 25.49.
[7] Department of Health, *Code of Practice: Mental Health Act 1983* (2008) para: 25.53.

The Responsible Clinician may decide that the patient requires a period of treatment in hospital and will therefore revoke the CTO. Before the CTO can be revoked, the Responsible Clinician and an AMHP must agree that that it is appropriate to revoke the CTO and that the patient meets the grounds for detention as set out in Section 3 of the 1983 Act – that is:

- He or she is suffering from a mental disorder of a nature or degree which makes it appropriate for him/her to receive medical treatment in hospital;

- It is necessary for the health or safety of the patient or for the protection of other persons that the patient should receive such treatment and it cannot be provided unless he or she is detained in hospital under this Section; and

- Appropriate medical treatment is available.

If the CTO is revoked, the patient's detention under the original detaining section of the 1983 Act will be re-instated and a new detention period begins for the purposes of subsequent review and applications to the Tribunal. Where the CTO has been revoked, the Hospital Managers are required to refer a patient's case to the Tribunal for review as soon as is practicable.

If the CTO has not been revoked within the 72 hours, the patient must be discharged from inpatient detention but the CTO will remain in force.

Consent to treatment

Community patients with capacity to consent
Community patients with capacity to consent (who have not been recalled) can be given treatment only with their consent. Treatment can be given without their consent only if they are recalled to hospital.

Community patients without capacity to consent
Community patients without capacity to consent (who have not been recalled) can be given treatment if a donee of a Lasting Power of Attorney, a deputy who has been appointed by the Court of Protection, or the Court of Protection consents to the treatment on their behalf.

Community patients without capacity to consent (who have not been recalled) can also be given treatment, without anyone's consent, if:

1. The person authorised to give treatment has taken reasonable steps before giving the treatment to establish whether the patient lacks capacity to consent and when giving the treatment the person reasonably believes the patient lacks capacity to consent;

2. The patient does not object or it is not necessary to use force;

3. The person giving the treatment is the Approved Clinician in charge of the treatment or the treatment is being given under his/her direction; and

4. The treatment does not conflict with an Advance Decision or a valid decision made by a donee of a Lasting Power of Attorney, a deputy of the Court of Protection, or the Court of Protection.

Children and young people
Where the community patient is aged under 18 and has capacity to consent (and has not been recalled), the same rules apply as above for adult community patients – that is, treatment cannot be given without the patient's consent.

Where the community patient is aged under 18 and lacks capacity to consent (and has not been recalled), the rules are similar to those for adult community patients – except that:

• An Advance Decision will not be relevant – because under the Mental Capacity Act 2005 Advance Decisions are limited to people aged 18 and over;

• Decisions by a donee of a Lasting Power of Attorney, a deputy of the Court of Protection, or the Court of Protection will not apply to patients under the age of 16 – because the Mental Capacity Act 2005, from which these provisions arise, does not apply to under 16s.

Emergencies
In an emergency, treatment can be given to community patients who lack capacity to consent (who have not been recalled) – including children and

young people. This can take place only where:

1. There is a reasonable belief that the patient lacks capacity or is not competent to consent.

2. The treatment is immediately necessary to: (a) save the person's life; (b) prevent a serious deterioration of the patient's condition and is not irreversible; (c) alleviate serious suffering by the patient and is not irreversible or hazardous; or (d) prevent the patient from behaving violently or being a danger to him/herself or others, and the treatment represents the minimum interference necessary for that purpose and is not irreversible or hazardous.

3. If it is necessary to use force against the patient, the treatment needs to be given to prevent harm to the patient and is a proportionate response to the likelihood of the patient suffering harm and the seriousness of that harm.

Such treatment may be given even if it conflicts with an Advance Decision, or the decision of a donee of a Lasting Power of Attorney or a deputy of the Court of Protection.

Second opinions

All community patients (who have not been recalled) may be given certain treatments for mental disorder only if a Second Opinion Approved Doctor (SOAD) has certified that the treatment is appropriate, in accordance with the provisions of Part 4A of the Mental Health Act. This includes treatments such as medication and ECT.

In the case of medication, the certificate does not have to be in place immediately for a community patient – but must be in place within one month from when the patient leaves hospital or three months from when the medication was first given to the patient (whether the medication was given in the community or in hospital), whichever is later.

The SOAD must certify in writing that it is appropriate for the treatment to be given. He/she does not have to certify that the patient has or lacks capacity, nor whether the patient is consenting to treatment or refusing.

The SOAD may specify within the certificate that certain treatment can be given to the patient only if certain conditions are satisfied. For example, the SOAD can specify that a particular drug and dosage can be given only if the patient has capacity to consent and does consent to the particular treatment. The SOAD can also specify whether and which treatments can be given to the patient on recall to hospital and the circumstances in which the treatments can be given.

It is not necessary to meet the certification requirement before treatment can be given:

- In emergencies to a patient who has not been recalled;
- In the community where that patient consents to treatment; or
- For patients who lack capacity, where a donee of a Lasting Power of Attorney or deputy of the Court of Protection consents to it on the patient's behalf.

Recalled patients

On recall to hospital, treatment may be given without consent where a SOAD certificate is in place which specifies this treatment as being appropriate in the circumstances (i.e. it can be administered on recall). If not, treatment cannot be given on recall without a new certificate.

There are, however, two, exceptions to this:

1. Medication, where less than one month has passed since the patient was discharged from hospital and placed on SCT;

2. Where the certificate authorises the treatment, even though it does not authorise it to be given on recall, if discontinuing it would cause serious suffering to the patient.

Section 117 aftercare

A patient on SCT can be provided with aftercare under Section 117 of the Mental Health Act.

Discharge from SCT

The patient can be discharged from SCT by the following means:

- The Responsible Clinician can discharge the patient from SCT at any time;

- The patient's Nearest Relative can apply to the Hospital Managers for the patient to be discharged from SCT, giving at least 72 hours' notice. The discharge can be barred by the Responsible Clinician if, following the notification, the Responsible Clinician provides the Managers with a report certifying that if the patient were to be discharged from the CTO he/she would be likely to act in a manner dangerous to other persons or to him/herself;

- The patient has the right to apply to the Hospital Managers for discharge;

- The patient has the right to apply to the Tribunal.

A patient subject to a CTO may be received into Guardianship by an application made in the normal way. The effect will be to end the CTO and the underlying liability to detention.

Guardianship

Guardianship allows a patient to receive care outside hospital where it cannot be provided without the use of compulsory powers. It allows a nominated person or body to assume responsibility for the supervision of a patient's care in the community.

According to the *Code of Practice*, Guardianship:

- Provides an 'authoritative framework for working with a patient, with a minimum of constraint, to achieve as independent a life as possible within the community';[8] and

- Is social care-led and primarily focused on patients with welfare needs.[9]

Who can apply for Guardianship?

A Guardianship application must be based on written recommendations by two doctors and completed by an Approved Mental Health Professional (or by the patient's Nearest Relative, although in practice this rarely occurs).

---

[8] Department of Health, *Code of Practice: Mental Health Act 1983* (2008) para: 26.4.
[9] Department of Health, *Code of Practice: Mental Health Act 1983* (2008) para: 28.3.

Who can be the Guardian?

The Guardian can either be a local social services authority or any other person approved by the local authority (known as a private guardian). The *Code of Practice* provides guidance on the suitable qualities of a private guardian.[10] In the majority of cases, however, the Guardian will be the social services authority.

Eligibility

A Guardianship application may be made on the grounds that:

- The patient is 16 years of age and is suffering from a mental disorder of a nature or degree which warrants his/her reception into Guardianship; and

- It is necessary in the interests of the welfare of the patient or for the protection of other persons that the patient should be so received.

The *Code of Practice* suggests that Guardianship is most likely to be appropriate where:

- The person is thought likely to respond well to the authority and attention of a Guardian, and so be more willing to comply with necessary treatment and care for his/her mental disorder; or

- There is a particular need for someone to have authority to decide where the patient should live or to insist that doctors, Approved Mental Health Professionals or other people be given access to the patient.[11]

The application

The application is made to a local social services authority and must include the name of the Guardian. Where the Guardian is not a local social services authority, the application must be accompanied by a written statement that the person is willing to act as Guardian. The *Code of Practice*

---

[10] Department of Health, *Code of Practice: Mental Health Act 1983* (2008) paras: 26.22 to 26.23.
[11] Department of Health, *Code of Practice: Mental Health Act 1983* (2008) para: 26.8.

states that applications should be accompanied by a comprehensive care plan, established on the basis of multi-disciplinary discussions under the Care Programme Approach in England (or its equivalent).[12]

The powers of the Guardian

Section 8 of the Act sets out the three powers of the Guardian as follows:

1. To require the patient to live at a place specified by the Guardian;

2. To require the patient to attend at specified places and times for medical treatment, occupation, education or training;

3. To require access to the patient to be given at the place where he or she is living to a doctor or Approved Mental Health Professional.

Enforcement of Guardianship

Guardianship does not provide the legal authority to:

- Detain a patient;

- Give medical treatment in the absence of the patient's consent; or

- Use force to ensure that he or she complies with any of the conditions.

Guardianship does, however, give authority for a patient to be returned to the place where it has been specified he or she must live, should he/she go absent without the permission of the Guardian. This power can also be used to take patients for the first time to the place they are required to live.

Guardianship cannot be used to require a patient to reside in hospital except where it is necessary for a very short time in order to provide shelter whilst accommodation in the community is being arranged.[13]

The *Code of Practice* recommends that if the patient consistently resists the exercise of the Guardian's powers, it can normally be concluded that Guardianship is not the most appropriate form of care for that person and that it should be discharged.[14]

---

[12] Department of Health, *Code of Practice: Mental Health Act 1983* (2008) para: 26.19.
[13] Department of Health, *Code of Practice: Mental Health Act 1983* (2008) para: 26.33.

Overlap with the Mental Capacity Act 2005

Mental incapacity is not a necessary pre-requisite for Guardianship. Where patients lack the relevant decision-making capacity, the *Code of Practice* suggests that in some circumstances the Mental Capacity Act 2005 may provide an alternative to Guardianship. For example:

> *Where an adult is assessed as requiring residential care and they lack the capacity to make this decision, then the Mental Capacity Act 2005 may be more appropriate: for example, through section 5 (protection from liability for actions in relation to care and treatment); the decision of a donee of a Lasting Power of Attorney or the deputy of the Court of Protection; or the deprivation of liberty safeguards.[15] In unusual cases it may also be necessary to seek a best interests decision from the Court of Protection.[16]*

The reception of a patient into Guardianship does not affect the powers of a donee of a Lasting Power of Attorney or a deputy of the Court of Protection, but they will not be able to make decisions about where the person must reside, or any other decisions which conflict with those of the Guardian.

Where a deprivation of liberty has been authorised under the Mental Capacity Act 2005, then this would not cancel Guardianship but the *Code of Practice* recommends that the local social services authority should consider whether Guardianship remains necessary.

Section 117 aftercare

Guardianship does not, in itself, come under Section 117 of the Mental Health Act. However, Guardianship patients will be eligible for Section 117 aftercare services if they have previously been detained under Section 3 or one of the other relevant sections of the Mental Health Act.

Rights of appeal

A patient can appeal to the Tribunal against Guardianship.

---

[14] Department of Health, *Code of Practice: Mental Health Act 1983* (2008) para: 26.35.
[15] Department of Health, *Code of Practice: Mental Health Act 1983* (2008) paras: 26.11 and 26.12.
[16] Department of Health, *Code of Practice: Mental Health Act 1983* (2008) para: 26.13.
[17] Department of Health, *Code of Practice: Mental Health Act 1983* (2008) para: 26.30.

Time limits and termination of Guardianship

Guardianship initially lasts for up to six months and can be renewed for a further period of six months and then for yearly periods.

Guardianship can be discharged by the Responsible Clinician, the Tribunal, the local authority or the Nearest Relative.

Guardianship also terminates if the patient is detained under Section 3 of the Mental Health Act.

Section 17 leave of absence

Under Section 17 of the Mental Health Act, a Responsible Clinician can grant leave of absence to a detained patient. The main exceptions to this are restricted patients, who may be granted leave by the Responsible Clinician but only with the Secretary of State's approval (see chapter 10).

Leave of absence allows a detained patient to be temporarily absent from hospital where further inpatient treatment is still thought to be necessary. This can be:

- For a specified period or occasions (for example, leave might be granted to visit family or attend an appointment); or

- It could be longer term or even an indefinite period (for example, to see how the patient copes with life outside of hospital).

However, it cannot go beyond the renewal date for the section.

Leave of absence may be granted subject to such conditions as are considered to be necessary. This might, for example, include a requirement to attend a medical centre to receive treatment or to reside at a particular place.

Consent to treatment

A patient who is on leave, continues to be liable to be detained, and therefore subject to the consent to treatment provisions in Part 4 of the Mental Health Act. The *Code of Practice* advises that, should it be necessary to treat the patient without his or her consent, then consideration should be given to recalling him or her to hospital – although this is not a legal requirement.[18]

Section 117 aftercare

The duty on local authorities and NHS bodies to provide aftercare under Section 117 of the Mental Health Act to certain categories of patients, also applies when they are on Section 17 leave.

Recall from leave

The Responsible Clinician may revoke a patient's leave at any time, in writing, if he or she considers this to be necessary in the interests of the patient's health or safety or for the protection of other people. This can be by force if necessary using a warrant to enter premises issued by a magistrate under Section 135(2).

A patient may not be recalled to hospital for the sole purpose of renewing the detention.

Relationship with SCT

Before granting long-term leave of absence (this is defined as over seven consecutive days), the Mental Health Act provides that the Responsible Clinician must first consider whether the patient should be dealt with under SCT. This requirement does not in practice apply to patients, such as those under Section 2 of the Act who are not eligible for SCT.

---

[18] Department of Health, *Code of Practice: Mental Health Act 1983* (2008) para: 21.24.

Chapter 8

Aftercare

Section 117 of the Act sets out a joint duty on health and social care services, in cooperation with voluntary agencies, to provide aftercare.

The term 'aftercare' is a misnomer left over from the days when mental healthcare was mainly given in hospitals. In modern services, the vast majority of mental health treatment is delivered to patients in the community. Admission is the exception and community care the norm.

Aftercare has unfortunate resonance with the word 'afterthought'. Yet to focus on inpatient care to the detriment of management in the community is to allow the tail to wag the dog in a way that increases risks for patients and staff alike. Most criticism in homicide inquiries is directed at community care rather than inpatient management or discharge decisions; and the period following discharge is one of the times of highest risk for suicide.

It is wrong to single out any part of the Act as more important than another. However, it is fair to say that it is when using those parts of the Act dealing with aftercare that professionals are most likely to find their actions subjected to later, hostile scrutiny. All the benefits of a costly admission may be lost if there is inadequate planning of aftercare.

Duty to provide aftercare

Aftercare for all patients should be planned within the framework of the

Care Programme Approach (see page 123), but for detained patients there are statutory entitlements under Section 117.

Section 117 applies to:

- All patients detained under Sections 3, 37, 45A, 47 or 48 of the Act;
  - When they cease to be detained; or
  - When granted leave of absence under Section 17; or
  - When placed on Supervised Community Treatment (SCT); and
- Patients who remain in hospital voluntarily after ceasing to be detained, once they leave; and
- Patients released from prison having spent part of their sentence detained in hospital under a relevant Section of the Act.

In all these circumstances, Section 117 obliges Primary Care Trusts (PCTs) and local social services authorities (LSSAs) to provide aftercare to patients. There is no time limit on the obligation. The duty to provide aftercare continues:

- For as long as the patient needs the service, including
- For the entire period of SCT in all cases, and
- After the cessation of SCT when necessary.

Although the duty to provide aftercare begins when the patient leaves hospital, the planning should begin immediately after admission.[1] PCTs and LSSAs should be involved at an early stage in identifying appropriate services. The same principles apply even in that small number of patients for whom admission is likely to be prolonged. The early establishment of a care pathway gives the patient concrete aims to keep in mind to help sustain motivation; and it helps services to avoid drift and the unnecessary prolongation of an admission.

Whilst PCTs and LSSAs are under an obligation to provide services, a patient is under no obligation to accept them. Any decisions they make should be fully informed. Willingness to accept a service should always be distinguished from need for that service and it is important to make that

[1] Department of Health, *Code of Practice: Mental Health Act 1983* (2008) para: 27.8.

distinction in records. A refusal to accept a service should not prevent a patient from receiving it at a later stage if there is a change of mind.[2] When a service has been declined, it is good clinical practice to review the need at subsequent care planning meetings and to offer it again if it is still needed.

Nature of the legal duty

The courts have interpreted Section 117 as imposing a strong duty on health and local authorities to arrange aftercare services, which are owed to and enforceable by individuals.[3] This means that in principle it can be enforced by an individual patient in the event of non-performance of the duty.

Once it has been decided that a patient needs specific services under Section 117, then there is a duty on the authorities to provide the service in question irrespective of resource considerations. This means that health or social services cannot refuse to make suitable aftercare arrangements on the sole ground of lack of resources.

However, in some cases the courts have accepted that there may be practical difficulties in carrying out this duty – for example, if there are no places available in the required residential care. In these types of cases, it is accepted that mental health services must use their best endeavours to arrange suitable aftercare services.[4]

Charging for Section 117 services

Under community care legislation, local authorities are entitled to charge service users for most services that are provided (both residential and non-residential). There are also some health services that are subject to a charge, such as prescriptions.

The courts have decided that it is unlawful to make charges for services provided under Section 117.[5] This is because Section 117 is seen as a

---

[2] Department of Health, *Code of Practice: Mental Health Act 1983* (2008) para: 27.22.
[3] *R v Ealing District Health Authority ex p Fox* [1993] 1 WLR 373.
[4] *R (IH) v Secretary of State for the Home Department* [2003] UKHL 59.
[5] *R v Manchester CC ex p Stennett* [2002] UKHL 34.

free-standing duty and is not a gateway provision that leads to services being provided under other statutes (which are subject to the charging regime). It follows that, since Section 117 does not include a charging provision, it is not permissible to charge for Section 117 services.

It should be stressed that this only applies to Section 117 aftercare. Patients who are not under Section 117 – for example, patients detained under Section 2 of the Mental Health Act or informal patients – can be charged for services.

The nature and purpose of Section 117 services

PCTs or LSSAs may provide services directly as well as commissioning them from others, including voluntary agencies.

The objectives of service provision are:

- To meet health and social care needs arising from a mental disorder;
- To support the patient in regaining, enhancing or learning skills to cope with life outside hospital and aimed at reducing that person's chance of being re-admitted to hospital for treatment for a mental disorder.

Types of Section 117 services

The term 'aftercare services' is not defined in the 1983 Act but case law has established a wide definition that includes:

social work, support in helping the ex-patient with problems of employment, accommodation or family relationships, the provision of domiciliary services and the use of day centre and residential facilities.[6]

The *Code of Practice* also lists a number of services that can be provided, including daytime activities, employment, accommodation, outpatient treatment, counselling, personal support, assistance with welfare rights, and financial assistance.

---

[6] *Clunis v Camden and Islington Health Authority* [1998] 3 All ER 180.

Planning aftercare

The Responsible Clinician preparing for:

- Discharge; or
- Leave of absence; or
- Transfer to SCT

should arrange:

- Assessment of aftercare needs;
- Discussion of those needs with the patient; and
- Updating of the care plan to address those needs.

The process may be adapted and abbreviated for short periods of leave, but no stage should be omitted. Even the shortest period of leave represents a significant transition for a detained patient and is therefore a time of heightened risk.

Who should be involved?

The list begins with the patient and, if applicable:

- An Independent Mental Health Advocate (IMHA);
- An Independent Mental Capacity Advocate (IMCA);
- The patient's attorney (appointed under a Lasting Power of Attorney) or deputy (appointed by the Court of Protection); and
- A solicitor or any other representative nominated by the patient.

In addition, the list may include, subject to the patient's consent in some cases:

- The Responsible Clinician, a nurse and other professionals from the inpatient team;
- A social worker;
- Members of the community team – for example, a doctor, nurse, clinical psychologist or other professional;
- The patient's GP and primary care team;

- Future carers; and

- Representatives of relevant voluntary organisations.

The list is not exhaustive and membership should be dictated by the patient's needs. Common additions are:

- The probation service in the case of a restricted patient;

- A representative of a housing authority; and

- An occupational or rehabilitation specialist.

The specific individuals involved should have the authority to take decisions regarding their own involvement and, as far as possible, that of their agency.[7] If approval needs to be obtained from more senior levels, steps should be taken to avoid delay in the implementation of the aftercare plan. In practice this means starting the process as soon after admission as possible.

Issues to be addressed:

The issues to be addressed will include where relevant:[8]

- Continuing mental health care, including medication;

- The psychological needs of the patient;

- The psychological needs of the family and carers;

- Physical healthcare;

- Daytime activity or employment;

- Accommodation;

- Risks and safety;

- Co-existing physical or mental disability;

- Needs associated with drug or alcohol use;

- Any parenting or caring needs;

- Social, cultural or spiritual needs;

---

[7] Department of Health, *Code of Practice: Mental Health Act 1983* (2008) para: 27.15.
[8] Department of Health, *Code of Practice: Mental Health Act 1983* (2008) para: 27.13.

- Counselling and personal support;

- Assistance in welfare rights and managing finances;

- The need to involve additional agencies – for example, probation or voluntary organisations; and

- Contingency plans and crisis contact details.

In addition to these general considerations, there will be a need to involve authorities and agencies in a different area if the patient is relocating.

Offender patients

Aftercare planning for a restricted patient must take account of any conditions imposed on a conditional discharge. Contingency planning is particularly important in these cases.

Any plans for accommodation should take into account any victims (and families of victims) of the patient's offence(s) where applicable. The location of accommodation may be subject to conditions in the case of a restricted patient but professionals should be sensitive to the needs of victims, even when no such conditions apply.

Aftercare planning in practice

The tasks for the professionals in collaboration and discussion with the patient are to:

- Establish an agreed assessment of needs;

- Develop a care plan;

- Agree a timescale for implementation of the various aspects of the care plan;

- Identify the people with specific responsibilities for implementation;

- Set a date for review;

- Record these arrangements;

- Supply a written summary to the patient and others who need it;

- Review regularly.

Any changes to the agreed plan should be made only after discussion with the patient and others involved, except in an emergency.

The responsibility for arranging reviews of the plan lies with the care co-ordinator.

The '117 Meeting'

This term is commonly used to refer to a care-planning meeting called to bring together the professionals involved to complete aftercare planning. It is also used to refer to subsequent review meetings.

It is essential to hold such a meeting, but the meeting alone does not fulfil the statutory obligations in respect of aftercare. Most of the necessary work has to be done in advance of the meeting, beginning as soon after admission as possible.

Tribunals and Hospital Managers

In order to review detention, the Tribunal and Hospital Managers need information on what aftercare arrangements could be made for the patient if he/she were to be discharged. Such information is essential; it is impossible to evaluate the case for continued detention/compulsion in order to manage risk without knowing how the risk would be managed if the patient were to be discharged.

There should be discussion of aftercare needs, involving LSSAs and other relevant agencies, before any hearing.[9] In practice, the best way of ensuring such a discussion takes place and is recorded is by holding a 117 Meeting before the hearing.

Where a Tribunal or Hospital Managers' hearing has been arranged for a patient entitled to aftercare under Section 117, the Hospital Managers should ensure that the relevant PCT and LSSA have been informed.[10]

The PCT and LSSA should consider making preparations for aftercare in every case, but particularly when discharge is likely if appropriate aftercare can be put in place.

---

[9] Department of Health, *Code of Practice: Mental Health Act 1983* (2008) para: 27.7.
[10] Department of Health, *Code of Practice: Mental Health Act 1983* (2008) para: 27.9.

There is a balance to be struck here. On the one hand, it is wasteful of resources to make elaborate aftercare arrangements for a patient who is unlikely to be discharged; but on the other hand, the discharge of a detained patient should never be delayed because of a failure to make aftercare arrangements.

Where the Tribunal decides to give a restricted patient a conditional discharge, the PCT and LSSA are obliged to take all reasonable steps to arrange aftercare that will allow the discharge to take place.[11]

Ending aftercare

The duty to provide aftercare services continues until both the PCT and the LSSA are satisfied the patient no longer needs them. The most straightforward case is when the person's mental health has improved so much that services are no longer needed. The patient (and relatives or carers as appropriate) should be fully involved in the decision. Great caution should be exercised before withdrawing services against the wishes of a patient; it would be sensible to seek a second opinion in an attempt to defuse conflict in such a case.

Aftercare services should not be withdrawn solely on the grounds that:[12]

- The patient has been discharged from the care of specialist mental health services;
- An arbitrary period of time has passed;
- The patient is deprived of his/her liberty under the Mental Capacity Act 2005;
- The patient is admitted to hospital voluntarily or under Section 2; or
- The patient is no longer on SCT or Section 17 leave.

A patient who is well and settled in the community may still need aftercare services to prevent a relapse or further deterioration.

---

[11] Department of Health, *Code of Practice: Mental Health Act 1983* (2008) para: 27.9.
[12] Department of Health, *Code of Practice: Mental Health Act 1983* (2008) para: 27.20.

Other forms of support

As noted above, Section 117 states a specific legal duty to provide aftercare services to some (but not all) patients who have been detained under the Mental Health Act. However, there are other forms of support available to mental health patients who have left hospital. These are summarised below.

Community care services

Under Section 47 of the NHS and Community Care Act 1990, social services are under a duty to carry out a community-care assessment where it appears that the person may be in need of services. This will include people who have been detained under the Mental Health Act 1983. The purpose of the assessment is to decide whether or not services should be provided to the person. This could include services under any of the following legislation:

Section 21 of the National Assistance Act 1948
This places a duty on local authorities to provide residential accommodation to people in need of care and attention which is not otherwise available to them.

Section 29 of the National Assistance Act 1948
This enables non-residential services to be provided to disabled people. This specifically includes people with a mental disorder.

Section 2 of the Chronically Sick and Disabled Persons Act 1970
This places a duty on local authorities to provide certain services to disabled people. This uses the same definition as Section 29 of the National Assistance Act.

The NHS Act 2006 and the NHS (Wales) Act 2006
This enables community services to be provided to people who are ill, and it specifically places a duty on local authorities to provide a number of services to people with a mental disorder.

The Health and Social Care Act 2001
This places a duty on local authorities to provide direct payments to service

users in certain circumstances. Direct payments enable people to purchase their own community care services rather than having the services arranged by social services. Direct payments can be provided to people detained under the Mental Health Act, subject to Supervised Community Treatment, Guardianship, leave of absence and conditional discharge. They can also be provided to people who lack capacity to consent to them, as long as there is an appropriate person to manage them on the patient's behalf.

Carers (Recognition and Services) Act 1995 and Carers and Disabled Children Act 2000

This legislation enables carers of people with mental health problems to be assessed for services.

Charging

As noted above, in most cases local authorities can charge service users for the provision of these services. However, this does not apply to Section 117 services.

Care Programme Approach

The Care Programme Approach (CPA) was established in 1991 in the joint Health and Social Services Circular HC(90)23/LASSL(90)11. It requires health authorities, in collaboration with social services departments, to put in place specified arrangements for the care and treatment of mentally ill people in the community. There are some differences to the application of CPA in Wales, but the principles are the same.

There are four distinct aspects to the CPA:

1. Assessment: Systematic arrangements for assessing the health and social needs of people accepted by the specialist mental health services;

2. A care plan: The formation of a care plan which addresses the identified health and social care needs;

3. Care coordinator: The appointment of a care coordinator to keep in close touch with the person and monitor care; and

4. Regular review, and if need be, agreed changes to the care plan.

The relevant guidance in England sets out a statement of values and principles:[13]

> *the approach to individuals' care and support puts them at the centre and promotes social inclusion and recovery. It is respectful – building confidence in individuals with an understanding of their strengths, goals and aspirations as well as their needs and difficulties. It recognises the individual as a person first and patient/service user second.*

> *Care assessment and planning views a person 'in the round', seeing and supporting them in their individual diverse roles and the needs they have, including: family; parenting; relationships; housing; employment; leisure; education; creativity; spirituality; self-management and self-nurture; with the aim of optimising mental and physical health and well-being.*

> *Self-care is promoted and supported wherever possible. Action is taken to encourage independence and self-determination to help people maintain control over their own support and care.*

> *Carers form a vital part of the support required to aid a person's recovery. Their own needs should also be recognised and supported.*

> *Services should be organised and delivered in ways that promote and co-ordinate helpful and purposeful mental health practice based on fulfilling therapeutic relationships and partnerships between the people involved. These relationships involve shared listening, communicating, understanding, clarification, and organisation of diverse opinion to deliver valued, appropriate, equitable and coordinated care. The quality of the relationship between service user and the care coordinator is one of the most important determinants of success.*

> *Care planning is underpinned by long-term engagement, requiring trust, team work and commitment. It is the daily work of mental health services and supporting partner agencies, not just the planned occasions where people meet for reviews.*

---

[13] Department of Health, *Refocusing the Care Programme Approach* (2008).

Chapter 9

Children and Young People

Introduction

For the purposes of this chapter:

- 'children' are defined as less than 16 years old; and

- 'young people' are those aged 16 or 17 years.

There is no minimum age limit for detention in hospital under the Mental Health Act. The main themes of this chapter are:

- Alternatives to using the Act, including the relevance of other legislation;

- Special considerations when applying the Act to children or young people; and

- Capacity and consent to treatment.

Other legislation

The Act never operates in isolation and even in adults it is necessary to bear in mind other legislation such as the Mental Capacity Act 2005 (MCA) and the Human Rights Act 1998. In children and young people, the list of relevant legislation expands to include the Children Acts 1989 and 2004, the Family Law Reform Act 1969, and the United Nations Convention on the Rights of the Child, as well as relevant case law, common law principles and codes of practice.

Those assessing and treating children and young people will need to be familiar with this other legislation. See *The Legal Aspects of the Care and Treatment of Children and Young People with Mental Disorder*[1] for further information.

Detailed consideration of the relevant legislation is beyond the scope of this chapter, which sets out some of the principles and questions that need to be borne in mind, such as:

- The concepts of parental responsibility and the parental zone of control;

- When to use the Mental Health Act and when to use the Children Act 1989;

- The meaning of capacity and consent in children and young people;

- How to make decisions about informal admission or treatment in young people;

- Children as informal patients;

- How the Mental Health Act regulates treatment for patients under 18;

- When to make an application to the court;

- Age-appropriate services;

- Applications and references to the Tribunal; and

- General duties relating to children and young people in hospital.

General principles

When taking decisions relating to the Mental Health Act:

- The best interests of the child or young person are always important and in many circumstances will override all other considerations;

---

[1] *The Legal Aspects of the Care and Treatment of Children and Young People with Mental Disorder: A Guide for Professionals.* London: National Institute for Mental Health in England (NIMHE) 2009.

- Keep the child or young person fully informed using age-appropriate information;
- Consider and document the child or young person's views, wishes and feelings;
- Choose the least restrictive intervention that is appropriate in the circumstances;
- Minimise separation from family, carers, friends and community;
- Ensure access to education.

Children and young people have the same rights to privacy, confidentiality and respect to dignity as do older people.

Summary of key points

If admission is informal:

- Age 16+, use Section 131 of the Mental Health Act;
- Age <16, obtain consent from a parent or person with parental responsbility.

If the young person agrees to admission:

- Age 16+, capacity can be presumed;
- Age <16, assess competence to consent.

If the young person is 16+ and has capacity, refusal cannot be overridden.

If <16, he/she can consent if competent but it is usual to get parental consent.

If <16 but not competent, the child cannot consent.

If <16, even competent refusal can be overridden by parental authority, the local authority, or the High Court; **but** the *Code of Practice* emphasises the trend towards increasing recognition of greater autonomy for children and young people.

Parental responsibility and consent to treatment

Children and young people can consent in some circumstances but in others consent is needed from a person with parental responsibility. Although not a legal requirement, it is good practice to involve both parents.

Problems arise when there is disagreement. If one person with parental responsibility disagrees with another over a decision to treat and is likely to challenge the decision in court, it is best to seek authorisation from the court before proceeding.

It is important to establish who has parental responsibility; it may not be a parent and it is sometimes the local authority.

Parental responsibility

Parental responsibility usually lies with the parents – but not always. When taking decisions under the Mental Health Act, it is essential to be certain where parental responsibility lies.

It is essential to know if any of the following apply as they may affect parental responsibility:

- Care order;
- Residence or contact order;
- Appointment of a Guardian;
- Parental responsibility agreement or order under Section 4 of the Children Act;
- Any order under wardship.

In a child or young person looked after by the local authority:

- If voluntarily accommodated ('voluntary care') parental responsibility is unaffected, that is, it remains with the parent or other person with parental responsibility who agreed to the arrangement.
- If a care order is in force, parental responsibility is shared with

the local authority and there will be agreement between them on who should be consulted about decisions. The local authority has powers to limit the extent to which parents or others with parental responsibility may exercise their parental responsibility[2] when such limits are in the best interests of the child or young person.

Once parental responsibility has been established there are two further considerations:

- Whether the person with parental responsibility has the capacity, within the meaning of the Mental Capacity Act 2005, to take a decision about the child or young person's treatment; and

- Whether the decision is within the zone of parental control (see below).

Zone of parental control

This new concept derives mainly from judgments made by the European Court of Human Rights. Its status remains uncertain at present. In due course it may acquire greater importance but it is equally possible that it will fade from the scene.

For the time being, the concept is intended to set limits on the extent to which a person with parental responsibility may consent to treatment on behalf of a child or young person. These limits apply in any and all situations – that is, over and above any conditions set by the Mental Health Act.

A decision falls within the 'zone of parental control' if it passes two tests:

- It should be a decision one would expect a parent to make, taking account of societal conventions and human rights law ('appropriateness'); and

- There should be nothing to suggest the parent may not be acting in the child's or young person's best interests.

The boundaries are not clearly defined. In all cases, it is necessary to consider:

---

[2] Children Act 1989, Section 33(3)(b).

- The age, maturity and understanding of the child/young person – the better equipped the child/young person is to take a decision, the less appropriate it is for somebody else to take it;

- Resistance from the child/young person.

In the specific case of mental health treatment, it is necessary to consider the invasiveness and/or restrictiveness of an intervention – the greater they are, the more likely it is the decision falls outside the zone. Examples would include any medication with severe side-effects; any treatment involving deprivation of liberty; and 'controversial' treatments. There is a specific exclusion of ECT. A decision on treatment may fall outside the zone of parental control simply because the proposed treatment is particularly invasive, restrictive or controversial.

A conflict of interest may be most apparent when there is a history of the person with parental responsibility having acted against the child/young person's best interests.

Less clear-cut examples include parental separation and conflict, when mutual parental hostility may impair the ability to make an impartial decision about the child.

When consent cannot be obtained

If, for any of the reasons outlined above, it is not possible to rely on the consent of a person with parental responsibility (for the purposes of treating mental illness) or on that of the child or young person, it is necessary to consider other options, namely:

- An application for detention under the Mental Health Act but only if all criteria for detention are met; or

- To seek authorisation from the court; or

- To use the Children Act so parental responsibility comes to lie with the local authority.

The role of the High Court

The High Court provides a means of legitimising decisions about admission or treatment in circumstances where it is not appropriate to use the Mental Health Act, and the Mental Capacity Act does not help. This is a specialist area and legal advice should be sought at an early stage. By definition, such problems fall outside the scope of the present text because the Mental Health Act does not provide a solution. Nevertheless, the basic principles are worth noting.

An application to the High Court should be considered in a child under 16 who is not 'Gillick competent' (see page 135) when:

- The person with parental responsibility cannot be identified or is incapacitated;

- There is strong disagreement between persons with parental responsibility;

- The person with parental responsibility may not be acting in the best interests of the child;

- The decision is not within the zone of parental control, for example, consent to ECT.

In a child who is Gillick competent, or in a capable young person, the only reason to consider an application to the High Court is to challenge a refusal of treatment. This is likely to be an extremely rare occurrence in mental health as the first response in such cases would be to consider using the Mental Health Act.

Specific references to possible use of the High Court are included at relevant points in this chapter.

Detaining a child or young person: Mental Health Act or Children Act?

If a child or young person with a mental disorder needs to be detained:

- Use the Mental Health Act when the primary purpose of detention is to provide medical treatment for mental disorder – for example, in the case of a child who is seriously mentally ill.

- Consider using Section 25 of the Children Act 1989 if the primary purpose is not to provide medical treatment for mental disorder, for example, when there is behavioural disturbance but no need for hospitalisation and secure accommodation is more appropriate.

Decisions on admission and treatment of 16-18 year-olds

At least one of the people involved in the assessment of a person who is under 18 years old, that is, one of the two medical practitioners or the Approved Mental Health Professional (AMHP), should be a clinician specialising in Child and Adolescence Mental Health Services (CAMHS).[3] When this is not possible, a CAMHS clinician should be consulted as soon as possible. Other specialists should be involved if the case is complicated by co-morbid conditions such as learning difficulties.

Informal admission and treatment of 16 or 17 year-olds

The law is different for young people and for children (under 16-year-olds), but in both cases the question of capacity to consent is of central importance.

- By virtue of Section 8 of the Family Law Reform Act 1969, young people aged 16 or 17 years old are presumed to be capable of consenting to their own medical treatment. The presumption applies to informal patients in hospital in exactly the same way as it applies to young people outside hospital. Capacity may of course be lost in particular circumstances.

- Section 8 applies only to the young person's own treatment. It would not apply to any treatment for research or other purpose that is not potentially of direct health benefit to the young person.

- Whilst the capacity to consent to non-therapeutic research is not presumed, it may be possible; the test is that the young person must have the understanding and ability to consent.

---

[3] Department of Health, *Code of Practice: Mental Health Act 1983* (2008) para: 36.20.

Young people with capacity to consent

Informal admission

Section 131 of the Mental Health Act allows that a 16- or 17-year-old with capacity may consent to, or refuse, admission irrespective of the wishes of a person with parental responsibility. A person with parental responsibility cannot consent on the young person's behalf. The young person is for this purpose in the same position as an adult except that, in certain circumstances, refusal to consent may be overridden by a court.

If the young person does not consent and admission is considered necessary, there are two options:

- Detention under the Act if the criteria are satisfied;

- To seek the authority of a court to treat against the young person's will.

Treatment

The criteria for assessing whether a young person is capable of consent are the same as those used for adults.

There is no legal necessity to obtain the additional consent of a person with parental responsibility, but it is good practice to involve the young person's family in the process, subject to the young person's consent to sharing of information.

As for an adult, consent is valid only when freely given and properly informed.

Unlike in an adult, the young person's refusal to consent may be overridden by a court in certain circumstances.

The position with regard to the overriding of consent is as follows:

- When a young person refuses consent, the courts have allowed a person with parental responsibility to overrule that refusal in non-emergency cases.

- All such decisions predated the Human Rights Act 1998.

- The general trend in the courts has been to allow greater autonomy for young people.

- The Department of Health believes it is unwise to rely on the consent of a person with parental responsibility to treat a young person who refuses in these circumstances.

- Consideration should be given to whether the criteria for detention under the Mental Health Act are met.

- If the criteria for detention are not met, it is probably best to seek authorisation from the court.[4]

In an emergency, it is likely the young person's decision would be overruled by a court and the clinician can act without anyone's consent if the refusal would be likely to lead to death or severe permanent injury.[5]

Young people who lack capacity to consent

Informal admission

- Section 131 of the Act does not apply to a young person who lacks capacity.

- The Mental Capacity Act applies in the same way as it does to adults unless the admission and treatment amount to a deprivation of liberty.[6]

- If there is a deprivation of liberty, admission cannot be authorised under the Mental Capacity Act; the legality of any such admission depends on common law principles.[7]

- Common law principles allow a person with parental responsibility to consent so long as the matter is within the zone of parental control.

- If outside the zone of parental control, consideration should be given to whether the criteria for detention under the Mental Health Act are met.

---

[4] Department of Health, *Code of Practice: Mental Health Act 1983* (2008) para: 36.33.
[5] Department of Health, *Code of Practice: Mental Health Act 1983* (2008) para: 36.34.
[6] Department of Health, *Code of Practice: Mental Health Act 1983* (2008) para: 36.35.
[7] Department of Health, *Code of Practice: Mental Health Act 1983* (2008) para: 36.36.

- If the Act is not applicable, it is necessary to seek authorisation from the court.[8]

Informal treatment

The situation is the same as for informal admission:

- The Mental Capacity Act applies in the same way as it does to adults unless the treatment amounts to a deprivation of liberty.

- If there is deprivation of liberty, it cannot be authorised under the Mental Capacity Act and common law principles apply.

- Common law principles also apply if the young person has capacity as defined in the Mental Capacity Act but for some other reason is incapable of consenting, for example, if overwhelmed by the implications of the decision.[9]

- A person with parental responsibility can consent on the patient's behalf if the matter is within the zone of parental control.

- If outside the zone of parental control, then consideration should be given to whether the criteria for detention under the Mental Health Act are met.

- If not, it is necessary to seek authorisation from the court.

Children under 16 years old

Competence

The term 'competence' is used in children in much the same way as 'capacity' is used in those aged 16 years and over. A child has the competence to consent to an intervention if he or she has sufficient understanding and intelligence to be able to comprehend fully what is involved.

Competence is sometimes referred to as 'Gillick competence' after the landmark case[10] which related to consent to oral contraception. The

---

[8] Department of Health, *Code of Practice: Mental Health Act 1983* (2008) para: 36.37.
[9] Department of Health, *Code of Practice: Mental Health Act 1983* (2008) para: 36.37.
[10] *Gillick v West Norfolk and Wisbech Area Health Authority* [1986] A.C.112.

concept is applicable to any form of medical treatment, including admission to hospital, as well as medical research or any other activity that requires the participant's consent.

Competence may vary according to:

- The child's age and maturity;
- The child's level of cognitive and emotional development;
- The complexity and nature of the intervention; and, of course,
- Mental disorder.

As the child develops, the likelihood of being competent in respect of a particular decision increases. However, the fluctuation in mental state as a consequence of mental illness may mean the child is competent at some times but not at others. The *Code of Practice* advises that in such cases of fluctuating competence, one should be cautious and consider whether the child is ever truly competent.[11] (It is arguable that the same consideration should apply to capacity in adults when the mental state fluctuates as a consequence of chronic mental illness.)

If a child is competent and consents to treatment, there is no legal requirement for additional consent by a person with parental responsibility. However, it is good practice to involve the child's parents, guardian or carers in the decision-making. In practice, it is difficult if not impossible to treat a child with severe mental health problems if there is a wide difference of opinion about treatment between the child and the person with parental responsibility. The latter has overall responsibility for the child's well-being and it is unrealistic to expect him or her to cooperate in a treatment they do not believe to be in the child's best interests.

Similarly, whilst one must seek the child's consent to the sharing of information about treatment, the emphasis is rather different from that in adults. The expectation would be that information is shared with the person who has parental responsibility.

Informal admission and treatment of a competent child

A competent child may consent to informal admission and/or treatment.

---

[11] Department of Health, *Code of Practice: Mental Health Act 1983* (2008) para: 36.40.

Consent should be sought for each element of treatment rather than seeking blanket consent.

If a competent child refuses admission for treatment, the situation is similar to that for a young person with capacity:

- The courts have allowed a person with parental responsibility to overrule that refusal in non-emergency cases; but

- All such decisions predated the Human Rights Act; and

- The general trend in the courts has been to allow greater autonomy for young people; so

- Consideration should be given to whether the criteria for detention under the Mental Health Act are met; and

- If the criteria for detention are not met it is probably best to seek authorisation from the court.[12]

In an emergency it is likely the competent child's decision would be overruled by a court and the clinician can act without anyone's consent if the refusal would be likely to lead to death or severe permanent injury.

Informal admission and treatment of a non-competent child

If the decision falls within the zone of parental control, a person with parental responsibility can consent on the child's behalf to informal admission to hospital for treatment of mental disorder.

The child's views should still be taken into account. The weight given to those views will depend on:

- The child's level of maturity; and

- Any views expressed before competence was lost (in the case of a fluctuating mental state).

Views expressed before losing competence may limit the zone of parental control when seeking consent from a person with parental control – for

---

[12] Department of Health, *Code of Practice: Mental Health Act 1983* (2008) para: 36.44.

example, if the child has expressed strong wishes not to be given a particular treatment.[13]

Consent to admission by a person with parental responsibility is not consent to all components of a treatment programme. Separate consent should be sought for all elements of the child's care and treatment.

If the decision is not within the zone of parental control, or if a person with parental responsibility does not consent:

- Informal admission and/or treatment is not possible;
- Consider detention under the Act if the criteria are met; and if not
- Consider seeking authorisation from the court.

Emergency treatment for children and young people

A life-threatening emergency may arise when:

- A capable patient refuses consent; or
- There is no time to seek the consent of a person with parental responsibility; or
- A person with parental responsibility refuses consent and there is no time to seek authorisation from the court.

In such cases, the courts have stated doubt should be resolved in favour of the preservation of life. Treatment may be undertaken without consent:

- To preserve life; or
- To prevent irreversible serious deterioration of the patient's condition.

---

[13] Department of Health, *Code of Practice: Mental Health Act 1983* (2008) para: 36.47

Treatments for children and young people regulated by the Mental Health Act

As with adults, the Act regulates treatments for mental disorder:

- In detained patients;
- In patients on Supervised Community Treatment (SCT);
- In informal patients for some specific treatments.

Specific treatments: Sections 57 & 58A

For treatments covered by Section 57 (mainly neurosurgery for mental disorder), treatment can be given only with the patient's consent irrespective of whether the patient is detained.

- Such treatment can never be given to a patient who lacks capacity/competence; and
- A person with parental responsibility cannot consent on the patient's behalf.

For treatment covered by Section 58A (electro-convulsive therapy, or 'ECT', at present, although other treatments may be added in the future) the Act applies to detained and informal patients.

- A detained, capable patient cannot be given ECT without his/her consent except in emergency.
- In emergency, or if the patient is incapable of consenting, treatment may be given without consent subject to certain conditions (see chapter 3).
- SCT patients must be recalled to hospital before treatment can be given without consent, even in an emergency.

Except in an emergency, a patient under 18 years may be given ECT only with the approval of a Second Opinion Appointed Doctor (SOAD) even if he or she consents. If a child or young person:

- lacks the ability to consent and
- is neither detained nor an SCT patient,

the Act contains nothing to prevent a person with parental responsibility consenting to ECT on his or her behalf. In practice, the authorisation of a court should be sought because, although there is no directly relevant case law, it is likely the decision to consent to ECT in such circumstances would lie outside the parental zone of control.[14] The exception would be a person of 16 or 17 years for whom the Mental Capacity Act could be used to provide the necessary authority so long as no deprivation of liberty was involved. In all cases, a SOAD certificate would still be needed except in emergency.

Children and young people who are not detained under the Act but may require ECT are eligible for access to Independent Mental Health Advocates.[15]

Other treatments

For detained and SCT patients of all ages, the normal provisions of the Act relating to consent are applicable. There is no requirement for people with parental responsibility to consent on behalf of children and young people in this position.[16]

Supervised Community Treatment

There is no lower age limit for SCT, although the numbers of children and young people subject to SCT are likely to be small.

Parents (or other people with parental responsibility) have no right of consent/refusal in relation to treatment for mental disorder whilst the child or young person is subject to SCT.[17] In practice, it would be difficult if not impossible to manage treatment under SCT if the child or young person lived with a person who did not approve of the treatment. There should always be ongoing consultation with the parents.

---

[14] Department of Health, *Code of Practice: Mental Health Act 1983* (2008) paras: 36.59 & 36.60.

[15] Department of Health, *Code of Practice: Mental Health Act 1983* (2008) para: 36.62.

[16] Department of Health, *Code of Practice: Mental Health Act 1983* (2008) para: 36.63.

[17] Department of Health, *Code of Practice: Mental Health Act 1983* (2008) para: 36.64.

[18] Mental Health Act 1983 (2008) Section 131A.

Age-appropriate services

Children and young people admitted to hospital for treatment of mental disorder must be accommodated in an 'age-appropriate' environment subject to any limitations imposed by their mental health or other needs.[18] Because of the resource implications, the duty to comply came into force in April 2010.

The age-appropriate environment includes:

- The physical environment;

- Staff training, skills and knowledge. Wherever possible care should be provided by specialists in the field; when that is not possible, there should be access to, and use of, specialist advice.

- The hospital regime, including mixing with and receiving visits from individuals of a similar age; and age-appropriate activities;

- Access to educational opportunities equal to that of their peers.

In practice, this usually means a dedicated child or adolescent ward. In exceptional cases, arrangements may be made to provide facilities, security and staffing appropriate to the needs of the child or young person even if the accommodation is in an adult facility.

The Act allows limited flexibility. Safety considerations may take precedence, particularly in an emergency. The standards used to judge long-term accommodation are stricter than for short-term or emergency use.

Sometimes, after due consideration, it may be decided the best place for a person under 18 is an adult ward – for example:

- When the person's 18th birthday is approaching;

- When the young person expresses a preference for an adult ward.

Some children and young people present a risk to their peers. That fact alone does not justify treatment on an adult ward and steps must be taken to identify a suitable, age-appropriate facility.

All staff working with children and young people must have enhanced and up-to-date disclosure clearance from the Criminal Records Bureau.[19]

---

[19] Department of Health, *Code of Practice: Mental Health Act 1983* (2008) para: 36.70.

Rights to apply to the Tribunal

The rights of children and young people detained under the Act are the same as those of older patients. However, Hospital Managers have a duty to refer cases to the Tribunal every year in under-18s rather than every three years as in adult patients.

Confidentiality

Like older patients, children and young people have a right to confidentiality but additional qualifications and limitations apply to that right. The younger the child, the greater will be the expectation that information will be shared appropriately.

Young people aged 16 or 17 and Gillick-competent children generally have the same rights to confidentiality as adults. In some circumstances, the duty of care to the patient may require confidentiality to be breached by providing information to those with parental responsibility. Just as in adults, the decision will often be complex and require the balancing of various risks and the duties to the parties involved.

As with any other decision, competence in relation to sharing information may change over time.

For further guidance in this complex and evolving area see the Royal College of Psychiatrists' guidelines.[20]

---

[20] CR133. *Good Psychiatric Practice: Confidentiality and Information Sharing.* London: Royal College of Psychiatrists, March 2006.

Chapter 10

Patients in Contact with the Criminal Justice System

Part 3 of the Mental Health Act 1983 concerns patients who are detained in hospital or received into Guardianship as a result of a court order. It also covers patients who are transferred to hospital or Guardianship from penal institutions, such as a prison, on the direction of the Secretary of State.

Other legislation is also relevant to people with mental health problems in the criminal justice system. This includes, for example, the law relating to the insanity defence, diminished responsibility and Community Rehabilitation Orders. The main provisions are summarised at the end of this chapter.

Diversion from the criminal justice system

As a general principle, people with mental health problems should be diverted from the criminal justice system in cases where the public interest does not require their prosecution. The purpose of diversion is to ensure that such people receive appropriate care and treatment from health and social services, and to provide advice to enable the courts to manage such cases appropriately.

The Mental Health Act *Code of Practice* states that people subject to criminal proceedings have 'the same right to psychiatric assessment and treatment as anyone else'.[1] This means that any person in prison or police custody or before the courts charged with a criminal offence, who needs medical treatment for mental disorder, 'should be considered for admission to hospital'.[2]

A number of services are normally available in police stations and magistrates' courts, to assess people with mental health problems and advise on their diversion from the criminal justice system.

Court diversion to hospital: Pre-sentence

The pre-sentence stage of criminal proceedings applies to people who are awaiting trial, or at any stage of a trial, or awaiting sentence. The Mental Health Act provides three main possibilities for dealing with people with mental health problems during the pre-sentence stage:

1. A court can remand an accused person to hospital for a report;

2. A court can remand an accused person to hospital for treatment; or

3. An accused person remanded in custody can be transferred to hospital.

These options are discussed in more detail below.

1. Remand to hospital for a report

Section 35 of the Mental Health Act allows a magistrates' court or the Crown Court to remand an accused person to hospital for the preparation of a report on his/her mental condition. This is an alternative to remanding the accused person in custody for a medical report, and is not an alternative to remand on bail.

When can this power be used?
In the Crown Court, this power applies to any person who is awaiting trial for an offence punishable with imprisonment or who is at any stage of such a trial prior to sentence. A remand to hospital cannot be made in respect

---

[1] Department of Health, *Code of Practice: Mental Health Act 1983* (2008) para: 33.2.
[2] Department of Health, *Code of Practice: Mental Health Act 1983* (2008) para: 33.2.

of a person convicted of murder, as a life sentence is mandatory. However, a remand for a report can be made in a murder trial before conviction.

In a magistrates' court, this power applies to any person convicted with an offence punishable on summary conviction with imprisonment or charged with such an offence. The court must be satisfied that the person did the act alleged or made the omission charged, or alternatively, the accused person may consent to the remand.

Criteria
The court must be satisfied, on the evidence of an Approved Clinician (oral or in writing) that the accused is suffering from a mental disorder and that it would be impracticable for a report on his/her mental condition to be made unless he/she were remanded on bail. There must also be evidence that arrangements have been made for the accused's admission to hospital and for this to take place within seven days.

Consent to Treatment
Part 4 provisions on consent to treatment do not apply. This means that the person is entitled to consent to, or refuse treatment in the same way as any informal patient.

The *Code of Practice* advises that where the person is in need of medical treatment under Part 4 of the Act, they should be referred back to court as soon as possible and if there is a delay in getting to court, consideration should be given to using Part 2 of the Act to allow compulsory treatment to be given.[3]

Time limits and termination
The remand is for a maximum of 28 days, although the court may renew this for further periods of 28 days to a maximum of 12 weeks.

The court may terminate the remand at any time. A patient remanded under this section is entitled to obtain a separate report from a doctor or an Approved Clinician, at their own expense, and to apply to the court on the basis of it for the remand to be terminated.

---

[3] Department of Health, *Code of Practice: Mental Health Act 1983* (2008) paras: 33.29 to 33.30.

2. Remand of accused person to hospital for treatment

Section 36 of the Mental Health Act allows the Crown Court to remand an accused person to hospital for treatment. This provides an alternative to the Secretary of State's power under Section 48 of the Mental Health Act to transfer unsentenced prisoners to hospital in an emergency (see below).

When can this power be used?
The power applies to a person who is in custody awaiting trial for an offence punishable with imprisonment (other than murder), or who is in custody at any stage of such a trial prior to sentence. It can also be used in cases where the defendant might otherwise be found unfit to plead, to enable him or her to receive treatment prior to trial, in order to allow the trial to proceed at a later date when his/her condition has improved.

Criteria
The Crown Court must be satisfied on the evidence of two doctors (oral or written) that:

- The person is suffering from a mental disorder of a nature or degree which makes it appropriate for him or her to be detained in hospital for treatment; and

- Appropriate medical treatment is available.

There also must be evidence that arrangements have been made for the accused's admission to hospital and for this to take place within seven days.

Consent to treatment
Part 4 provisions on consent to treatment apply. This means that some forms of medical treatment can be given to the detained patient without his/her consent in certain circumstances.

Time limits and termination
The remand lasts for a maximum of 28 days, although the court may renew this for further periods of 28 days, to a maximum of 12 weeks.

The court may terminate the remand at any time. A patient remanded under this Section is entitled to obtain a separate report from a doctor or an Approved Clinician, at his or her own expense, and to apply to the court on the basis of it for the remand to be terminated.

Court diversion to hospital: Sentencing options

When sentencing mentally disordered offenders, the court is bound by the requirement in Section 157 of the Criminal Justice Act 2003 to obtain a medical report before passing a custodial sentence other than one fixed by law. Before passing such a sentence, the court must consider any information before it which relates to the offender's mental condition and the likely effect of a custodial sentence on the offender's condition and on the treatment which may be available for it.[4]

1. Hospital Order

Section 37 of the Mental Health Act allows the Crown Court or magistrates' court to order the detention in hospital of certain categories of offenders. It is an alternative to a prison sentence for offenders who are found to be suffering from a mental disorder at the time of sentencing. No causal relationship has to be established between the offender's mental disorder and his/her offence.

When can this order be made?
The Crown Court may exercise this power where the defendant is convicted before the court for an offence punishable with imprisonment (other than murder).

In a magistrates' court, this power applies to any person convicted with an offence punishable on summary conviction with imprisonment, or a person charged with such an offence where the court is satisfied that the accused did the act or omission charged.

Criteria
The court must be satisfied on the evidence of two doctors that:

- The offender is suffering from a mental disorder that is of a nature or degree that makes it appropriate for him or her to be detained in hospital for medical treatment; and

- Appropriate medical treatment is available.

---

[4] Department of Health, *Code of Practice: Mental Health Act 1983* (2008) para: 33.17.

There must be evidence that arrangements have been made for the person's admission to hospital and for this to take place within 28 days. The court must also be satisfied that, having regard to all the circumstances, a Hospital Order is the most suitable method of dealing with the case.

Consent to treatment
Part 4 provisions on consent to treatment apply.

Time limits and termination
The Hospital Order can be for an initial period of up to six months with a first renewal period of six months and subsequent renewal periods of one year.

A patient may be discharged by the Responsible Clinician, the Hospital Managers or the Tribunal. The Nearest Relative does not have the power to order discharge but can apply to the the Tribunal.

2. Interim Hospital Order

If the court is uncertain that a full Hospital Order is appropriate, they can test this out by making an interim order under Section 38 of the Mental Health Act.

When can this order be made?
This power applies to the same categories of offenders as do Hospital Orders (see above) – but it does not apply to accused people before the magistrates' courts.

Criteria
The court must be satisfied, based on the evidence of two doctors, that:

- The offender is suffering from a mental disorder; and
- There is reason to suppose that the mental disorder is such that it may be appropriate for a Hospital Order to be made.

There must be evidence that the offender will be admitted within 28 days of the Order.

Consent to treatment
Part 4 provisions on consent to treatment apply.

Time limits and termination

This order can be made for up to 12 weeks in the first instance and can be renewed for periods of up to 28 days at a time, to a maximum of one year. If, following an Interim Order, a full Hospital Order is not deemed necessary, then the court can sentence the individual accordingly.

3. Restriction Order

Where the Crown Court makes a Hospital Order under Section 37 of the Act (see above), it may further order that the offender shall be subject to special restrictions in Section 41. The principal effect of a Restriction Order is that the patient cannot be given leave of absence or transferred to another hospital without the approval of the Secretary of State, and may not be discharged from hospital except by the Secretary of State or the Tribunal.

When can this order be made?

A Restriction Order can be made only if the court believes it is necessary to protect the public from serious harm, having regard to the nature of the offence, the antecedents of the offender and the risk of the offender committing further offences.

At least one of the doctors whose evidence is taken into account under Section 37 must give oral evidence to the court.

A magistrates' court has no power to make a Restriction Order but if it is satisfied that the conditions exist to make a Hospital Order, but it also feels a Restriction Order should be made, it may commit the offender (if over 14 years old) to the Crown Court, under Section 43 of the Act. Section 44 provides that the magistrate may direct that the offender be detained in any hospital to which arrangements have been made to admit him/her, pending the hearing of the case by the Crown Court. A patient admitted to hospital under Section 44 is detained as if he/she were subject to a Hospital Order with a Restriction Order.

Time limits

A Restriction Order is made without limit of time and will remain in force until the patient is discharged by the Secretary of State or the Tribunal.

Discharge

The Secretary of State or the Tribunal can discharge a Restricted Patient absolutely or conditionally. If the patient is discharged conditionally, the conditions usually imposed are those of:

- Residence at a stated address;
- Supervision by a social worker or probation officer – who would be required to submit regular reports to the Secretary of State on the patient's progress and to inform the Secretary of State (and the Responsible Clinician) if the patient's mental condition deteriorates; and/or
- Compliance with psychiatric treatment – including medication.

Reports from the Responsible Clinician and social supervisor must be submitted to the Ministry of Justice one month after discharge has taken place and at regular intervals thereafter – usually every three months.[5]

Recall
The Secretary of State may at any time while a Restriction Order is in force, order the recall of a conditionally discharged patient to hospital. Whether the Secretary of State decides to recall a patient depends largely on the advice of the Responsible Clinician, and the Secretary of State would normally be prepared to act on any such recommendation. The *Notes for the Guidance of Social Supervisors* state that it is not possible to specify all the circumstances in which the Secretary of State may decide to exercise this power, but in considering the recall of the patient he or she will always have regard to the safety of the public.[6]

Where a warrant is signed by the Secretary of State, the patient may be returned in the most appropriate manner to the hospital specified in the warrant. The consent to treatment provisions under Part 4 apply to the patient from the date of recall.

Termination of the Order
A Restriction Order ceases to have effect at the end of any period named in the Order by the Court, or may be brought to an end at any time by the Secretary of State. The patient is then treated as though he/she had been

---

[5] *Guidance for Social Supervisors – Supervision and After-Care of Conditionally Discharged Restricted Patients* (2007) Ministry of Justice, Department of Health, Welsh Office – para: 55.
[6] *Guidance for Social Supervisors – Supervision and After-Care of Conditionally Discharged Restricted Patients* (2007) Ministry of Justice, Department of Health, Welsh Office – para: 69.

admitted on a Hospital Order without restrictions (Section 37), made on the date the Restriction Order ceased to have effect.

A patient can apply to the Tribunal during the second six months of the detention, then once a year thereafter.

Mental Health Unit
The Mental Health Unit of the Ministry of Justice is responsible for carrying out the Secretary of State's responsibilities under the Mental Health Act 1983 and related legislation. In relation to restricted patients, this includes:

- Considering recommendations from Responsible Clinicians for leave, transfer and discharge;

- Preparing documentation for the Tribunal; and

- Where the patient has been conditionally discharged, monitoring the patient's progress and considering varying conditions, recall to hospital, or absolute discharge, as circumstances require.

4. Guardianship Order

Section 37 empowers the Crown Court or magistrates' court to place certain categories of offenders under the Guardianship of a local social services authority or of such other person approved by social services.

When can this order be made?
This order may be exercised by a Crown Court in cases where the defendant is convicted before that court for an offence punishable with imprisonment (other than murder).

Where the power is being exercised by the magistrates' court, it can be in respect of any person convicted by that court of an offence punishable on summary conviction with imprisonment or a person charged with such an offence where the court is satisfied that the accused did the act or omission charged.

Criteria

The court must be satisfied on the evidence of two doctors that the offender:

- Is suffering from a mental disorder; and

- Having reached the age of 16, the mental disorder is of a nature or degree which warrants his/her reception into Guardianship.

The court must also be satisfied that, having regard to all the circumstances, a Guardianship order is the most suitable method of dealing with the case.

The Guardian

The *Code of Practice* states that the court should be satisfied that the local authority or named person is willing to act as Guardian.[7] Section 39A requires a local social services authority to inform the court, if requested, if it or any other person is willing to receive the offender into Guardianship and how the Guardian's powers would be exercised.

Powers of the Guardian

The effect of the Order is to give the Guardian the power to:

- Require the offender to live in a specific place;

- Require the offender to attend specific places at specified times for medical treatment, occupation, education, or training; or

- Require access to the offender to be given at the place where the offender is living to any doctor, approved social worker, or other person specified by the Guardian.

Consent to treatment

A person placed on a Guardianship Order is not subject to the consent to treatment provisions contained in Part 4 of the Act.

Discharge

Orders can be discharged by the Guardian and the Tribunal. Nearest Relatives cannot discharge patients from Section 37 Guardianship Orders but they can apply to the Tribunal instead.

---

[7] Department of Health, *Code of Practice: Mental Health Act 1983* (2008) para: 26.32.

5. Hospital and Limitation Directions

Where the Crown Court, having considered making a Hospital Order (Section 37), instead imposes a fixed-term sentence of imprisonment, it may direct the immediate admission of the offender to hospital under Section 45A of the 1983 Act (a 'Hospital Direction'), together with a direction that the offender be subject to the special restrictions in Section 41 of the Act (a 'Limitation Direction').

Criteria
The court must have considered making a Hospital Order before it decides to impose a sentence of imprisonment. It must be based on the evidence of two doctors that:

- The person is suffering from a mental disorder of a nature or degree which makes it appropriate for him/her to be detained in hospital for medical treatment; and

- Appropriate treatment is available.

Admission to hospital must take place within 28 days.

Consent to treatment
Part 4 provisions on consent to treatment apply.

Discharge
Before the end of the prison sentence, the offender can be discharged only by the Secretary of State, on the recommendation of the Responsible Clinician or the Tribunal. The Secretary of State may order a return to prison instead. At the end of the prison sentence (allowing for remission), the Limitation Direction ceases to have effect, and the offender is treated as if she or he were on a Hospital Direction (Section 37).

Transfers from prison to hospital

Consent to treatment in prisons

Prisons, including prison healthcare centres, are not included within the definition of a hospital for the purposes of the Mental Health Act. This means that compulsory medical treatment under the Mental Health Act cannot be provided in a prison, where treatment without consent can be provided only under the common law. However, prisoners can be transferred to hospital under the Mental Health Act, where compulsory care and treatment under the Act's powers can be provided (see below).

Transfers of sentenced prisoners

Section 47 allows the Secretary of State to order the transfer of a sentenced prisoner to hospital.

Criteria
This must be based on reports from two doctors that:

- The person is suffering from a mental disorder of a nature or degree to warrant it appropriate for him/her to be detained in a hospital for medical treatment; and

- Appropriate treatment is available.

The Secretary of State must be of the opinion, having regard to the public interest and all the circumstances, that it is expedient to direct the prisoner's transfer. Admission to hospital must take place within 14 days.

Consent to treatment
Part 4 provisions on consent to treatment apply.

Restriction Direction
The Secretary of State may (and in respect of some prisoners must) impose the Special Restrictions under Section 41. In practice, the Transfer Direction is almost always coupled with a Restriction Direction.

A Transfer Direction not accompanied by a Restriction Direction because it was never imposed or has expired is referred to as a 'notional Section 37'.

Time limits and termination
The transfer lasts for up to six months, renewable for a further six months, then for one year at a time. If the Secretary of State imposes a Restriction Direction, it continues in force until the earliest date on which the patient would have been released from prison with remission.

If no Restriction Direction has been imposed, the patient can be discharged by the Responsible Clinician, Hospital Managers or the Tribunal. Until the end of her or his prison sentence (allowing for remission), a patient under a Restriction Direction can be discharged only by the Secretary of State. A patient can apply to the Tribunal, but the Tribunal can only recommend to the Secretary of State that the patient be discharged. The Secretary of State may order a return to prison instead. At the end of the prison sentence (allowing for remission), the Restriction Direction ceases to have effect and the above provisions apply.

Transfers of unsentenced prisoners

Section 48 allows the Secretary of State to direct the transfer to hospital of certain categories of unsentenced prisoners, who are waiting for trial or sentence and have been remanded in custody. Different considerations apply to unsentenced prisoners (as opposed to sentenced prisoners under Section 47 – see below) who have been transferred to prison due to the need to bring them to court or otherwise resolve the proceedings in which they are involved.

Criteria
The Secretary of State must be satisfied by reports of two doctors that the person is:

- Suffering from a mental disorder of a nature or degree which makes it appropriate for him or her to be detained in a hospital for medical treatment; and
- Is in urgent need of such treatment; and that
- Appropriate medical treatment is available.

The prisoner must be admitted to hospital within 14 days, otherwise the Transfer Direction will cease to have effect.

Restriction Order
The Secretary of State may, and in respect of some prisoners must, impose the Special Restrictions under Section 41 (see below).

Consent to treatment
Part 4 provisions on consent to treatment apply.

Time limits and termination

The transfer lasts for up to six months, renewable for a further six months, then for one year at a time. If the Secretary of State imposes a Restriction Direction, it continues in force until the earliest date on which the patient would have been released from prison with remission.

If no Restriction Direction has been imposed, the patient can be discharged by the Responsible Clinician, Hospital Managers or the Tribunal. Until the end of her or his prison sentence (allowing for remission), a patient under a Restriction Direction can be discharged only by the Secretary of State. A patient can apply to the Tribunal, but the Tribunal can only recommend to the Secretary of State that the patient be discharged. The Secretary of State may order a return to prison instead. At the end of the prison sentence (allowing for remission), the Restriction Direction ceases to have effect and the above provisions apply.

Victims

The Domestic Violence, Crime and Victims Act 2004 gives rights to victims of sexual or violent offences where the offender has been transferred to hospital under Sections 37 or 47 (whether or not a Restriction Order has been made) or under a Hospital and Limitation Direction order under Section 45A.

Under this Act, probation board victim liaison officers are required to approach victims in these cases, and offer to provide information and representation in respect of decision making over discharge from hospital. This could include:

- Decisions over the terms of any conditional discharge; or
- Proposals to place the patient on Supervised Community Treatment and any conditions relating to contact with the victim or victim's family.

The Mental Health Act *Code of Practice* states that professionals should encourage mentally disordered patients to share information to enable victims and victims' families to be informed about progress.[8]

---

[8] Department of Health, *Code of Practice: Mental Health Act 1983* (2008) para: 18.19.

Other criminal justice provisions

Remand on bail

A defendant with mental health problems has the same general right to bail as any other defendant and under the Bail Act 1976 there is a general presumption in favour of remanding a person on bail. The bail conditions relevant for mentally disordered offenders may include:

- Residence at the home address – to ensure that the defendant stays in the community and receives outpatient treatment;
- Keeping appointments for medical treatment;
- Cooperating with the preparation of a medical report;
- Residence at a hospital as an informal patient.

Unfitness to plead

Under the Criminal Procedure (Insanity) Act 1964, as amended, a defendant before the Crown Court may be found unfit to plead. The issue for the court is whether the defendant is so mentally disordered as to be able to understand or follow a criminal trial.[9] This must be based on evidence from two doctors, at least one of whom must be approved under the Mental Health Act. If the defendant is found unfit to plead, a 'trial of the facts' is then held to determine if the jury is satisfied beyond reasonable doubt that the defendant committed the act or omission alleged. The disposal options for the court to deal with such persons are:

- A Hospital Direction with or without a Restriction Direction;
- A Supervision and Treatment Order; or
- Absolute discharge.

Insanity

To establish the defence of insanity, it must be proved that at the time of committing the act, the defendant was 'labouring under such a defect of

---

[9] *R v Pritchard* (1836) 7 C&P 303.

reason, from a disease of the mind, as to not know the nature and quality of the act he was doing, or if he did know it, that he did not know it was wrong.'[10] The insanity defence is rarely used and in practice only for murder and other serious offences. The Criminal Procedure (Insanity) Act 1964 provides that evidence of insanity is required from two or more doctors, at least one of whom must be approved under the Mental Health Act. The disposal options are the same as for unfitness to plead (see above).

Diminished responsibility

This partial defence is available only for murder and, if successfully pleaded, reduces the murder charge to manslaughter on the grounds of diminished responsibility. This means that the mandatory sentence of life imprisonment for murder is avoided. Section 2 of the Homicide Act 1957 provides that an offender will not be convicted of murder if he/she was suffering from such abnormality of mind as to substantially impair his/her mental responsibility for the acts and omissions. Medical evidence is required for this defence but the decision rests with the jury. The sentencing judge has wide discretion in cases of manslaughter, including:

- A Hospital Order; Community Rehabilitation Order; and

- A life prison sentence – which is not uncommon where a successful defence of diminished responsibility has been founded on a condition which is likely to continue.

Infanticide

In strict terms, infanticide is not a defence but a category of homicide. This offence under the Infanticide Act 1938 is committed when a mother kills her child under the age of one year, when the balance of her mind is disturbed by reason of her not having fully recovered from the effect of giving birth to the child, or by reason of the effect of the lactation consequent on the birth. The scale of punishment is the same as for manslaughter – but the most frequent outcome is a Community Rehabilitation Order (see next).

---

[10] The M'Naghten Rules which derive from the case of Daniel M'Naghten (1843) 10 Cl & F 200).

Community Rehabilitation Order

A Community Rehabilitation Order (formerly known as a 'Probation Order') is a community sentence requiring an offender to work under the supervision of the probation service to avoid further reoffending. It is made under Section 41 of the Powers of Criminal Courts (Sentencing) Act 2000. In the case of mentally disordered offenders, any condition for which the person accepts medical treatment from a psychiatrist is included.

Chapter 11

Police Powers

The Mental Health Act 1983 gives the police a number of powers in relation to the detention of people with mental health problems. These are mainly concerned with taking people with mental health problems to a place of safety or retaking patients who have absconded, back to hospital. Other legislation gives the police a number of options when they are dealing with a possible offender whom they think might be mentally disordered. These are summarised at the end of this chapter.

Power to remove a person from a public place to a place of safety

Under Section 136 of the Mental Health Act, a police officer can remove a person from a public place to a 'place of safety' (see definition below) if he or she considers that:

1. The person is suffering from a mental disorder;

2. The person is in immediate need of care or control; and

3. It is necessary to remove that person to a place of safety in the interests of that person or for the protection of other persons.

The person does not need to have committed, or be suspected of having committed, a criminal offence.

Purpose of this power
The person can be detained in a place of safety for up to 72 hours so that

he/she can be examined by a doctor and interviewed by an Approved Mental Health Professional in order that the necessary arrangements can be made for his/her treatment or care.

Rights of a person under Section 136

A person removed under Section 136 is considered to be 'arrested' for the purposes of the Police and Criminal Evidence Act 1984 (PACE). It follows that the police have the power to search the person and remove certain items. There may also be a need for an Appropriate Adult (see below) to be present.

If a police station is used as the place of safety, the person has the right of access to legal advice under PACE and they must be notified of his/her rights and entitlements, as required under the PACE Code of Practice C.[1]

Where a hospital is used as the place of safety, the person must be informed of his or her legal position and rights. The Mental Health Act *Code of Practice* also advises that access to legal advice should be facilitated whenever it is requested.[2]

Consent to treatment

Detention under Section 136 does not include any power to treat the person without his or her consent.

Time limit

A person can be detained for no more than 72 hours. This cannot be renewed nor does the law allow consecutive periods of detention under Section 136. The authority to detain under Section 136 also expires when it has been decided that no further arrangements are necessary for the person's care or treatment. For example, if the doctor's assessment concludes that the person is not mentally disordered, then the liability to detain under Section 136 ends.

Outcome of the assessment

There are a number of possible outcomes following a Section 136 assessment:

    1. Compulsory admission to hospital may be needed, in which

---

[1] Available for download: http://police.homeoffice.gov.uk/publications/operational-policing /previous-PACE-codes-2005/PACE_Chapter_C.pdf?view=Binary

[2] Department of Health, *Code of Practice: Mental Health Act 1983* (2008) para: 10.46.

an assessment under the Mental Health Act would need to be completed;

2. Where a person is subject to Supervised Community Treatment, leave of absence or conditional discharge, they may be recalled to hospital;

3. The person could be admitted to hospital voluntarily;

4. The person could be transferred to another place of safety; or

5. The person could be discharged and appropriate support provided in a community setting.

Section 136 makes it clear that both a doctor and an Approved Mental Health Professional should carry out an assessment. If the doctor arrives first, and concludes that hospital admission is not necessary but some other form of care or treatment is needed, an Approved Mental Health Professional should still see the person. Only if the doctor arrives first and concludes that the person is not mentally disordered, should he or she be released before the arrival of the Approved Mental Health Professional.

Powers to remove a person from private premises

Section 135 provides a magistrate with the power to issue a warrant authorising a police officer to enter premises, using force if necessary, in order to remove a mentally disordered person to a 'place of safety' (see definition below). The warrant is executed once entry has been gained to the premises by the police officer, either by force or where force is not necessary.

A Section 135 warrant does not give any authority to impose medical treatment.

There are two types of warrants under Section 135:

1. Removal of a person not liable to be detained under the Mental Health Act

Section 135(1) is used where there are concerns about a person who is subject to the provisions of the Mental Health Act.

Criteria

Evidence must be provided to a magistrate, by an Approved Mental Health Professional, that there is reasonable cause to suspect that a person believed to be suffering from a mental disorder:

(a) Has been, or is being, ill-treated, neglected or kept otherwise than under proper control; or

(b) Is unable to care for him/herself and is living alone.

Effect of a Section 135(1) warrant

Section 135(1) allows a person to be removed from the premises specified in the warrant and, if necessary, taken to a place of safety for up to 72 hours, with a view to making an application for detention under Part 2 of the Mental Health Act (that is, Sections 2 or 3) or other arrangements for his/her care or treatment.

Who must accompany the police officer?

When executing a Section 135(1) warrant a police officer must be accompanied by:

- An Approved Mental Health Professional; and

- A doctor.

2. Removal of a patient liable to be detained under the Mental Health Act

Section 135(2) is used where a person is liable to be detained under the Mental Health Act or is required to reside at a particular place – for example, under Guardianship or Supervised Community Treatment and has refused to return to hospital after a period of leave, or has absconded from hospital or the place he or she is required to live under Guardianship or Supervised Community Treatment.

Criteria

Evidence must be provided to a magistrate by a police officer or any other person authorised to take the patient to any place that:

- There is reasonable cause to believe the patient can be found on premises within the local area; and

- Admission to the premises has been refused or is likely to be refused.

Effect of a Section 135(2) warrant
The warrant allows the patient to be taken to hospital or any other place.

In the case of Supervised Community Treatment or Guardianship, the patient can also be taken or retaken to the place he or she is required to reside.

Who may accompany the police officer?
When executing a Section 135(2) warrant a police officer *may* be accompanied by:

- A doctor; and

- Any person authorised under the Mental Health Act to take or retake a patient. This includes any officer on the staff of the hospital; an Approved Mental Health Professional; the Responsible Clinician; or someone authorised by the Guardian or local authority (in the case of Guardianship).

Places of safety

A place of safety can be:

- Residential accommodation (for example, a care home) provided by a local social services authority under Part 3 of the National Assistance Act 1948;

- A hospital;

- A police station;

- An independent hospital or care home for people with mental health problems; or

- Any other suitable place where the occupier is willing temporarily to receive the patient (this could include a relative or friend of the patient).

The Mental Health Act *Code of Practice* states that a police station should be used as a place of safety only on an 'exceptional basis' and it would be preferable to use a hospital or other healthcare setting where mental health services are provided.[3]

Where a police station is used, the *Code* suggests that health and social care agencies should work with the police in supporting the care and welfare of the person while in police custody and assist in arranging, where appropriate, the transfer of the patient to a more suitable place of safety.[4]

Transfers between places of safety
A person removed to a place of safety can be transferred to one or more other places of safety within the 72-hour period. The person must be taken by a police office or Approved Mental Health Professional, or any person authorised by them.

A transfer can be made before an assessment, during an assessment or after an assessment has taken place and the person is waiting for any necessary arrangements for his/her care or treatment to be put in place. Except in an emergency, the agreement of an Approved Mental Health Professional, a doctor or another healthcare professional should be obtained before a transfer takes place. In some cases, the person may need to be assessed before a transfer goes ahead.

Rights of people detained at police stations as a place of safety
The PACE Code of Practice C applies to all people who have been detained in a police station under Sections 135 and 136 of the Mental Health Act. The police, therefore, have the power to search the person and remove certain items. There may also be a need for an Appropriate Adult (see below) to be present.

If a police station is used as the place of safety, the person may also have the right of access to legal advice under PACE and he or she must be notified of his/her rights and entitlements, as required under the PACE Code of Practice C.[5]

Where a hospital is used as the place of safety, the person must be informed of his or her legal position and rights. The Mental Health Act

---

[3] Department of Health, *Code of Practice: Mental Health Act 1983* (2008) para: 10.21.

[4] Department of Health, *Code of Practice: Mental Health Act 1983* (2008) para: 10.23.

[5] Available for download: http://police.homeoffice.gov.uk/publications/operational-policing/previous-PACE-codes-2005/PACE_Chapter_C.pdf?view=Binary

Code of Practice also advises that access to legal advice should be facilitated whenever it is requested.[6]

Police involvement in Mental Health Act assessments

The police are sometimes asked to assist during Mental Health Act assessments, particularly if an application has been made to detain a patient who is unwilling to be moved. In such cases, the Approved Mental Health Professional can give the police authority to convey the patient, which allows the police to transport the person against his or her will and using reasonable force if necessary.

Other relevant police powers

Powers of entry
Under Section 17 of PACE, a police officer can enter and search any premises to:

- Execute a warrant;

- Arrest a person for an arrestable offence;

- Recapture someone unlawfully at large whom he or she is pursuing; or

- Save life and limb; or

- Prevent serious damage to property.

There is also a common law power of the police to enter private premises without a warrant to prevent a breach of the peace.

Appropriate Adult
The role of the 'Appropriate Adult' was created by PACE, with the intention of further safeguarding the rights and welfare of young people and vulnerable adults in custody.

---

[6] Department of Health, *Code of Practice: Mental Health Act 1983* (2008) para: 10.46.

When a person is arrested and the police officer suspects, or has been informed in good faith, that the person has a mental disorder or is otherwise mentally vulnerable, an Appropriate Adult must be contacted and asked to attend the police station.

An Appropriate Adult can be:

- A relative, Guardian or other person responsible for the detained person's care or custody;

- Someone experienced in dealing with mentally disordered or mentally vulnerable people but who is not a police officer or employed by the police; or

- Failing these, some other responsible adult aged 18 or over who is not a police officer or employed by the police.

The key roles of the Appropriate Adult are:

- To support, advise and assist the detained person, particularly while he or she is being questioned;

- To observe whether the police are acting properly, fairly and with respect for the rights of the detained person;

- To assist with communication between the detained person and the police; and

- To ensure that the detained person understands his or her rights.

It is not the role of the Appropriate Adult to provide the detained person with legal advice or to encourage the vulnerable person to cooperate with the police.

The powers of the Appropriate Adult include the following:

- To be told why the detained person is being held;

- To speak to the detained person in private at any time;

- To inspect the written record of the person's period in detention (the custody record) at any time;

- To see copies of the notices of rights and entitlements referred to above;

- To see a copy of the PACE Codes of Practice setting out the powers, responsibilities and procedures of the police;

- To intervene in an interview if it is necessary and in the interests of the detained person to help him or her communicate effectively with the police; and

- To ask for a break in any interview, either to seek legal advice or to consult with the detained person (particularly if the interview is a lengthy one or if the detained person is distressed or ill).

The Appropriate Adult is entitled to be present during any procedure where information needs to be given by or sought from the detained person and also when any form of consent is sought from the detained person or he or she is asked to agree and/or sign any documentation. For example:

- When the custody officer informs the detained person of his/her rights and entitlements;

- When the detained person is cautioned;

- When the person is charged;

- Subject to strictly limited exceptions, during any search of the detained person involving removal of more than outer clothing;

- When the need to keep the person in detention is reviewed;

- During any form of identification procedure such as an identification parade;

- During any process involving the fingerprinting or photographing of the detained person or when a sample is taken from him/her.

Chapter 12

Risk Assessment and Management

One of the main changes in the 2007 revision of the Mental Health Act 1983 is the greater emphasis placed on risk assessment and management. The broader definition of mental disorder and removal of exclusion criteria mean decisions on compulsory treatment depend less on diagnosis and more on the risks involved.

The main arguments in favour of the change are:

- Psychiatric diagnosis is unreliable and prone to error; and
- A diagnostic label alone is almost worthless as an indicator of treatment needs.

The main concerns about this change are:

- The difficulty of assessing risk reliably and accurately; and
- Doubts about the ethics of risk assessment.

This chapter therefore addresses both the ethics and the practicalities of risk assessment.

Risk and safety

The risks with which the Act is concerned are:

- Self-neglect;

- Self-harm; and

- Violence to others.

For these purposes, violence to others includes any sexual activity to which the other person does not consent or to which the person is incapable of consenting. It includes all sexual activity between an adult and a child or young person below the age of 16.

When setting out the criteria for detention the Act refers to:

- The patient's health or safety; and

- The protection of others.

Reports written for Mental Health Act assessments should include the terms in the Act even if they also include discussions of risk in other terms.

Risk and safety are different sides of the same coin and should always be considered together. A comparison of the two terms helps to illustrate the ethical framework of risk management.

The ethics of risk and safety

Our dealings with people begin with an assumption of relative safety. We take general precautions, beginning with the injunction on children not to talk to strangers and extending to the use of metal detectors (for example, to detect knives) and other security screening in many public situations, but we assume there is no particular risk from an individual until we have evidence to the contrary. We assume also that we are dealing with a person who has autonomy and is able to look after his or her own best interests without assistance. Likewise the patient presenting to mental health services is entitled, within limits, to an assumption of autonomy and safety unless there is evidence of risk.

The assumption of safety has limited applicability when carrying out assessments under the Mental Health Act and it must always be balanced against the duty of care. In crisis situations, the circumstances alone may indicate risks to self or others. Also risk is intrinsic to many mental disorders; there are about 1300 patient suicides every year in England and Wales. In depression or other serious mental illness, the duty of care owed to the patient negates the usual assumption of safety and makes a risk assessment mandatory.

Much criticism of risk assessment focuses on stigma and the negative consequences of identifying risks. Yet the purpose of risk assessment is to discriminate between different levels of risk. If the process is effective it must be capable of indicating low risk or safety as well as high risk. Once the process is acknowledged as a measure of safety as well as risk, many of the ethical concerns melt away. In fact professionals have an ethical duty to take reasonable steps to demonstrate that a situation or management plan is safe, even though the process may identify risks that need to be addressed.

There is a genuine conflict of values involved in managing risk and it is best made explicit. The main values in conflict are:

- Respect for patient autonomy and a desire to minimise medical or other interference with the freedom of the individual; versus

- The rights of others to live safely and free from the fear of violence; and

- The rights of patients to be protected and treated when they are incapacitated by mental disorder.

The conflict of values cannot be avoided simply by stressing only one side of the argument. The challenge is to find ways of negotiating the conflict by acknowledging the opposing pressures and finding the best compromise.

The Mental Health Act encourages and facilitates the process by emphasising that consideration of the appropriateness of compulsory treatment must go beyond clinical matters to take into account all aspects of the case (see chapter 2). Even so, the need to reconcile these conflicting values is the greatest challenge in mental health care and there are no simple solutions. The best we can do is to set out some principles that should guide the process.

These principles are:

- The process of risk assessment should be transparent and open to scrutiny;

- Subject to the requirements of medical confidentiality, there should be wide consultation with interested parties, including potential victims, when deciding on the appropriateness of detention;

- Training and policies should be designed to ensure non-discriminatory practice;
- Preference should be given to the least restrictive alternative consistent with safety of the patient and other persons.

Despite the conflict of values there is plenty of common ground when dealing with the risk of harm to others. An act of serious violence has profound negative consequences for the patient as well as for the victim. The perpetrator may lose his/her liberty for a long time. He or she has to come to terms with having caused serious injury, often to a family member or loved one.

These dire consequences illustrate the fact that serious violence is one of the most important negative outcomes in mental disorder. Reasonable steps to prevent violence are part of the duty of care to the patient as well as being part of a more general obligation to protect others.

Principles of risk assessment and management

Although there are differences between assessments of risks for violence, self-harm and self-neglect, many of the principles are the same:

- The past is the best guide to the future;
- Risk is multi-dimensional;
- Risk is not a property of the individual alone;
- Risk changes with time;
- Relative estimates of risk are better than absolute measures;
- Risk is not the same as stated intent.

In the following discussion the term 'problem behaviour' is used to refer to all three of the risks above (self-neglect, self-harm and violence to others) unless it is necessary to make a distinction between them.

The past is the best guide to the future

The assessment of risk begins with:

- A detailed history; including

- Any previous occurrences of the problem behaviour; and

- A description of the internal and external factors associated with the problem behaviour.

The general principle is that risk is greater when:

- There have been problems in the past; and

- Present circumstances resemble the circumstances in which those problems occurred.

The ultimate aim is to intervene to change the circumstances and the outcome.

Of course, the future differs from the past. Human behaviour is not always consistent and it may be very inconsistent. Even so, the odds favour an assessment based on a detailed history.

In addition, the method can accommodate inconsistency; the evidence of past behaviour may be that in a future relapse there will be a high risk of impulsive, unpredictable actions. One can predict unpredictability and a high probability of impulsive risky behaviours should lead to caution in management.

A detailed history has a bearing on the assumption of safety. A serious suicide attempt during a previous episode of depression means safety cannot be assumed; in a present or future relapse it will be necessary to take steps to address the risk of suicide.

Hence the same mental state findings are interpreted differently according to the history. Given a diagnosis of depression and a similar mental state, the risk of self-harm is rated more highly when the patient has a history of self-harm. If a florid psychotic episode has been accompanied by violence in the past, it is reasonable to assume a similar episode will probably be accompanied by violence in the future.

An assessment under the Mental Health Act should include a history. When possible, the history given by the patient should be supplemented by records and the accounts of other informants. The extent to which this is necessary or possible will depend on the nature of the case and the seriousness of the risks involved. Different standards will apply if detention is prolonged, or in forensic rather than general settings.

Sometimes it is not possible to obtain records or reliable information. When it is necessary to take decisions based on incomplete information, it is essential to document the deficiencies and the steps taken to remedy them. In some circumstances, the Act allows for safe, interim actions whilst uncertainty is resolved – for example, use of Section 2 rather than Section 3 (see chapter 2).

In summary:

- A comprehensive risk assessment requires a full history;

- Present findings at interview can be correctly interpreted only in the light of the history;

- The history given by the patient should be supplemented by information from records and/or informants when possible;

- Any uncertainties or shortcomings in the available information should be documented.

Risk is multi-dimensional

Risk differs from properties like height or weight in two main ways:

- Risk is not an intrinsic property of the individual (see next section); and

- Risk is multi-dimensional and cannot be reduced to a score, percentage or number.

A comprehensive risk assessment leads to a description that may include the following:

- Nature – the types of problem behaviour;

- Severity – the seriousness of the consequences;

- Frequency – how often the behaviour is likely to occur;

- Imminence – the likely timescale;

- Probability – the likelihood of occurrence;

- Identity or nature of likely victims (violence risk only);

- Factors that increase or decrease the risk.

The list may seem over-ambitious but it is surprisingly easy to apply in clinical practice. This can be demonstrated in the following case examples.

Example 1

In emotionally unstable personality disorder, it is common to encounter deliberate self-harm that is consistent in nature and severity; occurs frequently; varies in imminences according to mental state and circumstances; and often has a high overall probability of occurrence based on the frequency with which it has happened in the past.

Example 2

A person with morbid jealousy may be very likely to attack his/her partner; moderately likely to attack a member of his/her family; and unlikely to attack a member of the general public. The violence may be life-threatening (dependent largely on history) and may be preceded by interrogation or verbal threats. Common factors that increase risk are: intoxication with alcohol and the development of depression, paranoia or other deterioration in the mental state. The above factors allow an estimate of imminence.

Example 3

A paedophilic sexual offender may present a high risk of sexual assault to children but a low risk of violence to other groups of people. The nature of the likely assaults is assessed mainly on the history of previous assaults, supplemented by information from the mental state examination, including sexual fantasies. Common factors increasing risk are: depression, alcohol use, increased level of sexual preoccupation, breakdown of adult relationships, and exposure to possible victims.

It follows from the above examples that risk cannot be reduced to a single dimension or percentage. A comprehensive risk assessment is a qualitative description of problem behaviours along with the likelihood of their occurrence and the factors that make them more or less likely to occur.

Risk is not an inherent property of the individual alone

The best way to understand this point is by comparing the discredited concept of dangerousness with current thinking about violence risk.

Although dangerousness is concerned only with violence to others, the same principles apply to self-harm and self-neglect.

Psychiatry abandoned the concept of dangerousness in favour of risk because the former emphasised individual characteristics to the exclusion of all else. Risk is not an inherent property of the individual but depends also on external circumstances and contingencies.

As dangerousness was inherent to the patient, the finding of dangerousness was often seen as the end of the story. By contrast, a description of risks ought to be the beginning of a process leading to safer management of the case.

The concept of dangerousness was insidious and damaging to patient care. When combined with the belief that certain disorders or patients were untreatable, it encouraged therapeutic nihilism; once the patient was labelled dangerous the only question was how to impose restrictions. The consequences could be serious when some patients were also regarded as untreatable.

These notions are surprisingly resistant to change. Some commentators use the term risk whilst retaining the old assumptions about dangerousness – that is, that it is intrinsic to the patient and the only possible responses are confinement or restraint.

When used correctly, the concept of risk management encourages therapeutic optimism. It allows us to sidestep concerns about whether a mental disorder is 'treatable'. The likelihood of a response to therapy is just one part of the equation and many other interventions can have a dramatic effect on risk.

The best example is probably the impact of alcohol or drug use on risk. Even when nothing more can be done to treat the core mental disorder, whether that disorder is schizophrenia or antisocial personality disorder, successful treatment of substance misuse may have a dramatic impact on risk.

Hence the assessment of substance misuse will form part of most assessments under the Mental Health Act. Whilst dependence on drugs or alcohol cannot be used as a basis for detention, substances are likely to be the commonest extrinsic risk factor considered in association with other mental disorders.

Risk changes with time

Once we recognise the relationship between risk and circumstances, the management of risk becomes a fluid, ongoing process rather than a static one. Assessment at any one point in time must look back at the history, but it is also necessary to look forward to how the risks may change in the future.

Assessments under the Mental Health Act inevitably involve an impending change in circumstances because, depending on the outcome, the patient may be leaving the hospital, clinic or other protected environment. The critical question concerns the risks the patient will present in the future which may be different from the risks he or she presents in the consulting room. Future risks may be affected by foreseeable stresses; access to drugs, alcohol or the means to self-harm; default from treatment; relapse; and access to potential victims.

The extent to which these factors influence the recommendation will vary according to the particular case. The discussion on the Historical Clinical Risk-20 below shows some of the factors to be considered in relation to past, present and future.

A common error in risk assessment is to place too much emphasis on the here and now rather than taking a longitudinal view of the case. The present mental state is important, but it needs to be considered in relation to the history and likely future circumstances.

Whilst some people undergo an assessment during brief or fleeting contact with services, for many patients an assessment under the Mental Health Act will be just one event in ongoing contact with services. The assessment and decision taken should make sense as part of the care pathway. Whether the decision is for or against compulsion, it should be part of a continuing care plan for risk management.

Relative estimates of risk are better than absolute measures

Risk changes with time and with circumstances. It is best described in terms of contingencies or conditional statements: if this or that condition applies the risk will be increased; if other conditions apply the risk will be reduced.

It is not usually helpful to attempt to reduce risk to an absolute measure such as a number or percentage. As risk is multidimensional, there would have to be more than one number. Even if it were possible to attach a number to a particular risk, that number may change dramatically with a change in circumstances. It is far more useful for the clinician to be aware of those factors that are likely to increase risk.

Conditional statements about risk should be based on the history as well as on general considerations. In general, it is safe to state that depression increases the risk of self-harm or suicide but an individual assessment may reveal concerns that are specific to the individual.

Because individual, personal concerns may be of overriding importance, the value of standardised approaches to risk assessment is limited. Ticking boxes next to a list can never be a substitute for a full history and understanding of the individual's life history.

Nevertheless, there are several factors that commonly increase the risks of self-harm, self-neglect or violence in mental disorder. They should probably be considered in all assessments under the Mental Health Act: They are:

- Relapse or deterioration of mental state;
- Non-compliance with treatment;
- Disengagement from treatment;
- Use of drugs or alcohol;
- Bereavement;
- Financial problems;
- Loss of employment;
- Breakdown of a relationship;
- Loss of accommodation/unstable accommodation.

Risk factors are additive but not in a simplistic way. The risk is increased if several of these factors apply, but in a particular case a single risk factor may be of critical importance even if none of the others applies. Standardised assessments cannot take account of such idiosyncrasies and there is no substitute for a detailed history and knowledge of the individual's life.

Risk is not the same as stated intent

One of the commonest errors in risk assessment is to rely on a single interview and mental state examination. The history is of central importance to the diagnosis and to risk assessment, but a single examination may also be an inadequate basis for assessment of mental state.

The main limitations of a single mental state examination are:

- Reluctance to disclose personal information;
- Suspiciousness caused by mental disorder;
- Lack of insight or self-knowledge.

A comprehensive risk assessment touches on intimate matters of (literally) life and death. It is not surprising that there is reluctance to talk openly about such matters at a first meeting with a stranger. The patient may be ashamed to talk about thoughts of suicide or other risks. He or she may be frightened of the consequences of revealing thoughts that might be recognised as 'abnormal'.

In addition to such normal reservations, mental disorders are often associated with fear and suspiciousness. The patient may doubt the interviewer's identity or motives. It is in precisely those cases where there is most loss of contact with reality that it may be most difficult for the interviewer to gain trust in order to have access to the patient's mental state.

Another problem associated with lack of insight is that a patient may not understand the impact of the mental disorder on his or her functioning. In some psychotic conditions there may be rapid fluctuations in mental state so expressions of intent have little or no value.

Severely depressed patients often struggle with self-destructive impulses for long periods of time; the fatal act requires only the briefest period of surrender to those impulses.

The other problem in severe mental illness is that the usual, assumed chain linking intention and action may be broken. The action may come first, with no warning thought or utterance. Even after the event the patient may be unable to articulate any understandable connection between thoughts and action.

In these circumstances there is no place for fine distinctions based on the patient's stated intentions. Of course those intentions should be taken into account, but the crucial question is the extent to which current circumstances resemble those in which there has been risky behaviour in the past.

In patients with no relevant past history, it is necessary to fall back on general considerations. Psychotic patients with violent or suicidal preoccupations need urgent treatment and they will usually need close observation until the treatment takes effect.

A framework for clinical assessment of risk

The table shows the various components of a comprehensive risk assessment. It was developed for assessment of violence risk but could easily be adapted for assessment of other risks.

Table 1: A framework for clinical risk assessment (from Gunn, 1993)[1]
1. Detailed life history
2. Substance abuse
3. Psychosexual assessment
4. Description of previous offending/antisocial behaviour
5. Psychological assessments
6. Mental state assessments
7. Attitude to treament/Insight

Most assessments under the Mental Health Act include only a tiny fraction of this information. Even so, the ideal is worth bearing in mind if only as a reminder to the clinician of what he or she does not know.

The standard of an assessment is judged according to what is reasonable in the circumstances. In practice, most assessments will include the following:

History including:

- Circumstances of presentation and reasons for assessment;
- A brief life history;

---

[1] Gunn J (1993) Dangerousness. In: Gunn J, Taylor PJ (eds) *Forensic Psychiatry. Clinical, legal and ethical issues.* London: Butterworth Heinemann, pages 624-645.

- Medical and psychiatric history;
- Previous self-harm or self-neglect;
- Previous violence and antisocial behaviour.

Mental state examination including:

- General demeanour including self-care;
- Signs and symptoms of psychosis or depression;
- Suicidal thoughts or intentions;
- Threats or hostility;
- Insight and attitudes to treatment;
- Future plans and intentions.

Supplemented by:

- Records when available;
- Information from carers, relations or other informants.

It is important to document any uncertainties or shortcomings in the information available, as well as steps taken to remedy the problem.

Structured assessments of risk

There has been a massive expansion of interest in structured risk assessment in recent years, mainly because large studies demonstrate its statistical superiority to unstructured clinical assessment.

The two main approaches to standardisation are:

- Actuarial or standardised risk assessment;
- Structured clinical assessment of risk.

Actuarial or standardised risk assessment

The term 'actuarial' is derived from the life insurance industry in which facts are gathered and combined to estimate the risk of death over a specified period of time. Actuarial assessment of violence risk is in direct contrast to unstructured clinical methods. There are strict rules about the data to be gathered and how the data are weighted and combined to give an assessment of violence risk.

The advantages are:

- Transparency;
- Minimisation of bias;
- Consistency;
- Good predictive accuracy in populations.

The disadvantages are:

- No room for discretion;
- It ignores all factors other than those specified;
- Poor prediction in individuals.

The actuarial approach is of limited value in assessments under the Mental Health Act because:

- The Act requires that assessments are tailored to the individual case; and
- Decisions on detention under the Act must take account of all the circumstances of the case.

Actuarial assessments may be used by specialist services to supplement a fuller clinical assessment. For example, the assessment of risk in sexual offending is ideally suited to the use of an actuarial measure such as the Static 99.[2]

Structured clinical assessment

The structured clinical method incorporates the positive aspects of actuarial assessment and unstructured clinical approaches.

A structured clinical assessment requires:

- The collection of specified data about the individual;
- The use of additional data at the clinician's discretion;

[2] Hanson RK, Thornton DM (2000) Improving risk assessments for sex offenders: a comparison of three actuarial scales, *Law and Human Behaviour*, 24, 1, 119-136.

- Flexibility in the use and interpretation of all the data to formulate a risk assessment.

The best known example is the Historical Clinical Risk-20 (HCR-20).[3] The HCR-20 requires the collection of 20 data items: 10 items are historical and refer to the past; five are clinical and relate to present state; and five risk management items relate to the future.

Table 2: The 20 Items of the HCR-20 (Webster et al, 1997)

Historical Items

    H1: Previous Violence

    H2: Young Age at First Violent Incident

    H3: Relationship Instability

    H4: Employment Problems

    H5: Substance Use Problems

    H6: Major Mental Illness

    H7: Psychopathy

    H8: Early Maladjustment

    H9: Personality Disorder

    H10: Prior Supervision Failure

Clinical Items

    C1: Lack of Insight

    C2: Negative Attitudes

    C3: Active Symptoms of Major Mental Illness

    C4: Impulsivity

    C5: Unresponsive to Treatment

Risk Management Items

    R1: Plans Lack Feasibility

    R2: Exposure to Destabilisers

    R3: Lack of Personal Support

    R4: Non-compliance with Remediation Attempts

    R5: Stress

---

[3] Webster CD, Douglas KS, Eaves D, Hart SD (1997) *HCR-20. Assessing risk for violence, Version 2.* Vancouver: Mental Health, Law and Policy Institute, Simon Fraser University.

With the basic data in place, the clinician adds idiosyncratic variables and formulates the risks. There is complete freedom to interpret the data as appropriate to the individual case.

The second stage of the HCR-20 is to formulate feared scenarios of violence based on the available data. For each scenario it is necessary to:

- Specify factors that will increase the risk;

- Specify protective factors that will decrease the risk;

- Suggest interventions; and

- Assign priority to the case.

The HCR-20's three strands relating to past, present and future are ideally suited to the Care Programme Approach framework. Given time, training and other resources, it is ideally suited to assessments under the Mental Health Act. It has already been widely adopted by specialist forensic services in England.[4] See Maden's *Treating Violence*[5] for a fuller discussion of standardised approaches to the assessment of violence risk.

Risk sharing and ownership

Risk can never be eliminated entirely. Clinicians have to deal with uncertainty. It is inevitable that things will sometimes go wrong so preparation for a bad outcome is part of risk management.

Risk assessment has three component questions:

- What are the risks associated with treatment of this mental disorder?

- How can the risks be reduced?

- Are the residual risks acceptable?

The first two questions are reasonable questions for mental health professionals because professional expertise is directly relevant. The third

---

[4] Khiroya R, Weaver T, Maden A (2009) The use and perceived utility of structured violence risk assessments in English medium secure forensic units. *Psychiatric Bulletin* 33: 129-132.
[5] Maden A (2007) *Treating violence: a guide to risk management in mental health.* Oxford: Oxford University Press.

question, about the acceptability of risk, is not a matter for technical expertise. It involves moral, social and philosophical considerations.

The Mental Health Act incorporates this principle in two ways:

- The Hospital Order with restrictions allows professionals to give their opinions on the risks but the responsibility for discharge rests with the Secretary of State for Justice or the Tribunal.

- In other patients the decision to detain must be appropriate in a general sense as well as clinically appropriate.

The implication is that doctors and other professionals should involve not only the full multidisciplinary team but also relations and carers whenever possible. When dealing with mentally disordered offenders, there may be joint working with the probation service or the involvement of the Multi-Agency Public Protection Panel. The common theme is a wider sharing of risks that go beyond purely medical considerations.

The second opinion

Risk assessments are rarely right or wrong in categorical terms. They vary in quality but it is not always simple to judge their quality.

There is usually room for discretion in the way risks are managed. There will often be several acceptable alternatives rather than a single right answer. So far as it is possible, it is desirable to share risks through multidisciplinary and multi-agency working.

Some decisions remain clinical in nature; lay opinion may not be appropriate or helpful. In complex cases the best course of action is to seek a second clinical opinion.

Greater use should be made of specialist or forensic services in this respect. There may be no expectation that the service will take over the patient, but the endorsement of current treatment can provide reassurance to clinician, patient, carers and relations.

Chapter 13

The Mental Capacity Act 2005

The Mental Capacity Act 2005 (MCA) covers England and Wales and came into force in 2007. It provides a statutory framework for adults who lack capacity to make decisions for themselves, or who have capacity and want to make preparations for a time when they may lack capacity in the future. Everyone working with and caring for adults who lack capacity, including health and social care professionals, family members and other carers, must comply with the MCA.

The MCA Code of Practice supports the MCA and provides guidance and information to all those working under the legislation.[1] Certain categories of people are required to have regard to the relevant guidance in the MCA Code of Practice, including anyone acting in a professional capacity.

The statutory principles

Section 1 of the MCA sets out five key principles that underpin the whole legislation and apply to all decisions and actions taken under the Act. According to the Code of Practice to the MCA, the message conveyed by these principles is intended to be enabling and supportive of people lacking capacity, not restrictive or controlling of their lives.[2] The statutory

---

[1] This can be downloaded from http://www.publicguardian.gov.uk/mca/code-of-practice.htm
[2] Department for Constitutional Affairs, *Mental Capacity Act 2005: Code of Practice* (2007) page 19.

principles can be summarised as follows:

1. **The presumption of capacity**: a person must be assumed to have capacity unless it is established that he or she lacks capacity (Section 1(2)).

2. **Maximising decision-making capacity**: a person is not to be treated as unable to make a decision unless all practical steps to help him or her to do so have been taken without success (Section 1(3)).

3. **Unwise decisions**: a person is not to be treated as unable to make a decision merely because he or she makes an unwise decision (Section 1(4)).

4. **Best interests**: an act done, or decision made, under this Act for or on behalf of a person who lacks capacity must be done, or made, in his or her best interests (Section1(5).)

5. **Least restrictive intervention**: before the act is done, or decision is made, regard must be had as to whether what is needed can be as effectively achieved in a way that is less restrictive of the person's rights and freedom of action (Section1(6)).

The MCA Code of Practice suggests that following these principles and applying them to the MCA's framework for decision making will help to ensure that appropriate action is taken in individual cases and point the way to solutions in difficult or uncertain situations.[3]

Assessing mental capacity

The definition of incapacity

Section 2 sets out that for the purpose of the MCA:

> ...*a person lacks capacity in relation to a matter if at the material time he is unable to make a decision for himself in relation to the matter, because of an impairment of, or a disturbance in the functioning of, the mind or brain.*

---

[3] Department for Constitutional Affairs, *Mental Capacity Act 2005: Code of Practice* (2007) page 19.

This definition reflects the principle that incapacity is 'decision specific' and must be assessed in relation to the particular decision that needs to be taken, not the person's ability to make decisions generally. It follows that a person may lack capacity in relation to one matter but not in relation to another. Thus a person may be able to make some decisions, such as deciding where to live or what clothes to wear on a particular day, but the same person may be unable to deal with complex matters such as managing a share portfolio or conducting legal proceedings.

Incapacity is also 'time specific' and must be assessed at the time the decision needs to be made. A person can lack capacity even if the loss of capacity is temporary – for example, while someone is under a general anaesthetic, or if the person's capacity fluctuates, may be because they have mental health problems that mean on some days or in some situations they are unable to make decisions.

Section 2(3) of the MCA makes it clear that a lack of capacity cannot be established merely by reference to a person's age, appearance, or any condition or aspect of a person's behaviour which might lead others to make unjustified assumptions about capacity.

The two-stage assessment of capacity

A two-stage test must be applied to decide whether an individual has capacity to make a particular decision – a 'diagnostic test' and a 'functional test'.[4]

Stage 1: Diagnostic test of capacity
The lack of capacity must be caused by an impairment or disturbance in the functioning of the mind or brain. This could cover a range of conditions such as psychiatric illness, learning disability, dementia, brain damage or drug and alcohol misuse.

Stage 2: Functional test of capacity
The second stage requires the assessor to show that the impairment or disturbance causes the person to be unable to make the decision in question. According to Section 3(1) of the MCA, a person is unable to make a decision if he/she cannot:

---

[4] Department for Constitutional Affairs, *Mental Capacity Act 2005: Code of Practice* (2007) page 19, para: 4.10.

1. Understand the information relevant to the decision;

2. Retain that information;

3. Use or weigh that information as part of the process of making the decision; or

4. Communicate his or her decision (whether by talking, using sign language or any other means).[5]

Who can assess capacity?

The MCA does not require that the assessment of capacity must be carried out by a doctor or other healthcare professional in every case. For most day-to-day actions or decisions, it will be sufficient for the carer most directly involved with the person at the time to make this assessment. The Code of Practice gives guidance as to when a professional assessment is likely to be required and, as a general rule, suggests that the more serious the decision, the more formal the assessment of capacity may need to be and an assessment of capacity by a professional might be necessary.[6]

Best interests

It is a key principle of the MCA that anything that is done, or any decision made, on behalf of a person who lacks capacity must be in that person's 'best interests'. This is a legal concept and Section 4 of the MCA provides a checklist of factors that decision-makers must work through in deciding what is in a person's best interests.

Section 4(1) of the MCA includes a clear statement that a determination of someone's best interests must not be based merely on the basis of the person's age or appearance, or any condition or aspect of his/her behaviour which might lead others to make unjustified assumptions about the person's best interests.

---

[5] Mental Capacity Act 2005 Section 3(1).
[6] Department for Constitutional Affairs, *Mental Capacity Act 2005: Code of Practice* (2007) page 19 paras: 4.38-4.43.

The best-interests checklist

The Code of Practice makes clear that this is not an exhaustive list but rather is a list of common factors that must always be considered in determining a person's best interests. The checklist is therefore just a starting point and in many cases extra factors will need to be considered.[7]

- First, the decision maker must consider whether it is likely that the person will at some time have capacity in relation to the matter and, if so, when that is likely to be. This allows for the possibility that the decision may be put off until the person has the capacity.

- Second, the decision maker must, as far as reasonably practicable, permit and encourage the person to participate, or improve his/her ability to participate as fully as possible in the decision-making process or in relation to any act done to him or her.

- Third, the decision maker must consider, as far as it is reasonably ascertainable:

  a) The person's past and present wishes (including any written statement made by him/her when he/she had capacity);

  b) The beliefs and values that would be likely to influence his/her decision if he/she had capacity; and

  c) The other factors that he/she would be likely to consider if he/she were able to do so.

- Fourth, the decision maker must, if it is practicable and appropriate to consult them, take into account the views of:

  a) Anyone named by the person as someone to be consulted on the matter in question or on matters of that kind;

  b) Anyone engaged in caring for the person or interested in his or her welfare;

  c) Any donee of a Lasting Power of Attorney granted by the person; and

  d) Any deputy appointed by the Court of Protection.

---

[7] Department for Constitutional Affairs, *Mental Capacity Act 2005: Code of Practice* (2007) page 19 para: 5.6.

Best interests and life-sustaining treatment

When the determination relates to life sustaining treatment, Section 4(5) of the MCA requires that the decision maker must not, in considering whether the treatment is in the best interests of the person concerned, be motivated by a desire to bring about his or her death.

Any decision relating to life-sustaining treatment, therefore, must be based on the best interests of the person concerned. It does not mean that doctors are under a duty to provide or continue to provide life-sustaining treatment where that treatment is not in the best interests of the person.[8]

Protection for those providing care or treatment

If a person has capacity then many actions, such as giving treatment or interfering with his/her property, might be unlawful if carried out without his/her consent. Where a person lacks capacity, the MCA allows health and social care professionals and informal carers to carry out certain tasks without incurring any legal liability.

Section 5 of the MCA specifies that a person providing care or treatment will not incur any liability if:

1) Reasonable steps are taken to establish whether the person lacks capacity in relation to the matter in question;

2) Consideration has been given to the principles of the MCA set out in Section 1; and

3) The action taken is in the person's best interests.

Actions which are not protected

There are a number of limitations on acts which are protected under Section 5 of the MCA.

---

[8] Department for Constitutional Affairs, *Mental Capacity Act 2005: Code of Practice* (2007) page 19 para: 5.33.

1. Deprivations of liberty

Actions which amount to a deprivation of liberty, within the meaning of Article 5(1) of the European Convention on Human Rights,[9] will not attract protection from liability, except in strict circumstances such as:

- When this has been authorised by the Court of Protection;

- Under the Deprivation of Liberty Safeguards (this is considered in more detail in the next chapter); or

- In order to provide life-sustaining treatment or any vital act while a decision is sought from the Court of Protection.

2. Restraint

Restraint under Section 5, is permitted only if the person using it reasonably believes it is necessary to prevent harm to the incapacitated person, and if the restraint used is proportionate to the likelihood and seriousness of the harm. The restraint must also be in the person's best interests. Section 6 of the MCA defines restraint as the use or threat of force where an incapacitated person resists, and any restriction of liberty or movement whether or not the person resists.

3. Advance decisions, attorneys and deputies

Section 5 does not authorise any act which conflicts with a valid advance decision or valid decision by an attorney acting under a Lasting Power of Attorney or a deputy appointed by the Court of Protection (see below).

Lasting Powers of Attorney

A Lasting Power of Attorney (LPA) enables a person over 18 (the donor) to appoint another person or persons (his or her donee or attorney) to act on his/her behalf if he/she subsequently loses capacity. This has replaced the Enduring Power of Attorney as the type of power of attorney which can operate after a person ceases to have capacity.

There are two types of LPA:

---

[9] Determining whether a deprivation of liberty has taken place is complex and covered in more detail in the next chapter.

1. A property and affairs LPA for decisions about financial and property matters. This type of LPA can be used while the donor still has capacity, unless he/she specifies that it can't.

2. A personal welfare LPA. This can be used only when the donor no longer has capacity to make the particular decision affecting his/her health or personal welfare.

For both types of LPA the donor is able to specify exactly what types of decision can be made for him/her, or he/she can give blanket permission for one or more attorneys to act on his/her behalf in relation to all issues covered in the LPA.

The Court of Protection has wide powers under the Act to determine questions and give directions as to the meaning and effect of an LPA. It can also remove attorneys who act improperly.

How to create an LPA

To create an LPA, donors need to fill in a form, which is available from the Office of the Public Guardian together with guidance on how to fill it in. There are two forms, one for each type of LPA. The form includes a certificate which must be signed by an independent person stating that the donor fully understands the power he or she is giving to the attorney and that he or she has not been put under pressure to do so. The LPA must then be registered (for a fee) with the Office of the Public Guardian before it can legally be used.

Role of the attorney

When acting under an LPA, the attorney is subject to the provisions of the MCA and in particular the principles of the MCA set out in Section 1 and the best interests requirement in Section 4. The attorney is also subject to common law duties and responsibilities, including a duty of care and a fiduciary duty.

Enduring Powers of Attorney

LPAs replaced Enduring Powers of Attorney (EPAs) and it is no longer possible to create a new EPA. However, those EPAs created before the MCA came into force on 1 October 2007, whether they have been registered or not, continue to be valid.

Advance Decisions to refuse treatment

Advance Decisions allow people with capacity to refuse specified medical treatment at a point in the future when they lack the capacity to consent to that treatment. Only people aged 18 and over, who have the capacity to do so, can make an Advance Decision. If an Advance Decision is both valid and applicable in the particular circumstances, it has the same effect as a contemporaneous refusal of treatment by a person with capacity. This means that the treatment specified in the decision cannot lawfully be given.

The MCA does not impose any particular formalities concerning the format of Advance Decisions or the procedures involved in making an Advance Decision, except for decisions relating to life-sustaining treatment (see below). Advance Decisions concerning the refusal of other types of treatment may be written or oral. The Code of Practice contains suggestions about what to include in a written Advance Decision and how, and how to record verbal Advance Decisions.[10]

The Court of Protection has the power to make declarations as to the existence, validity and applicability of an Advance Decision in relation to the treatment under consideration. The Court, however, has no power to overturn a valid and applicable Advance Decision.

Life-sustaining treatment

Advance Decisions relating to any treatment which a doctor considers necessary to sustain life must comply with a number of strict formalities set out in the MCA. These are that the Advance Decision must be in writing and be signed and witnessed. In addition, there must be an express statement that the decision stands 'even if life is at risk'.

Advance Statements

It is important to recognise that an Advance Decision to refuse treatment is not the same as an 'Advance Statement', which sets out a person's views about his/her care and treatment needs and preferences. For example, an

---

[10] Department for Constitutional Affairs, *Mental Capacity Act 2005: Code of Practice* (2007) page 19 paras: 9.10 to 9.23.

Advance Statement might include information about the type of medical treatment the person would like or where he or she would prefer to live, in the event of future incapacity. Advance Statements are not legally binding but should be taken into account by decision makers when making best interests determinations. If an Advance Statement is not followed, the Code of Practice advises that the reasons should be recorded.[11]

Independent Mental Capacity Advocate

The MCA provides for the appointment of an advocate, known as an Independent Mental Capacity Advocate (IMCA), to support a person who lacks capacity when certain important decisions are being made. In most cases, an IMCA is appointed for a person who lacks capacity where there is no one else who can speak for them and represent their views – such as family members or friends who are engaged in caring for the person (apart from paid or professional carers).

The role of the IMCA

The functions of the IMCA listed in section 36(2) of the MCA are:

1. Providing support to enable the person to participate as fully as possible in the decision;

2. Obtaining and evaluating relevant information;

3. Ascertaining and representing the person's wishes, feelings, beliefs and values;

4. Finding out about available options; and

5. Seeking further medical opinion if necessary.

The NHS body or local authority involved in the decision must take into account any information given or submissions made by the IMCA when determining what decision is in the best interests of the person lacking capacity.

The IMCA can challenge the decision-maker on behalf of the person

---

[11] Department for Constitutional Affairs, *Mental Capacity Act 2005: Code of Practice* (2007) page 19 para: 5.43.

lacking capacity if necessary. The IMCA can also access formal dispute resolution procedures – such as the complaints procedure – and in serious cases he or she can seek permission to refer the matter to the Court of Protection.

Serious medical treatment and the provision of long-term accommodation

An IMCA must be instructed for people lacking capacity who have no-one else to support them (other than paid staff) when decisions need to be taken about serious medical treatment and the provision of long-term residential accommodation. Such decisions could include:

- Whether to provide, withhold or withdraw serious medical treatment;
- Where it is proposed to move a person into long-term care in a hospital or care home; or
- Where a long-term move to a different hospital or care home is proposed.

Accommodation reviews

An IMCA may be instructed (but is not required to be instructed) for accommodation reviews for a person who lacks capacity where there is no other appropriate person to consult. This only applies in cases where the accommodation has been arranged by the local authority or the NHS and where it would be of particular benefit to the person concerned if an IMCA were instructed.

Adult protection cases

An IMCA may be instructed (but is not required to be instructed) in adult protection cases, whether or not family, friends or others are involved, where the local authority or the NHS is satisfied that it would be of particular benefit to the person concerned if an IMCA were instructed. This applies when protective measures are being put in place where a person who lacks capacity is being abused or neglected, or when he or she is alleged to be the abuser.

The Court of Protection

The Court of Protection lies at the heart of the MCA. It has jurisdiction relating to the whole Act and is the final arbiter for capacity matters.

The Court of Protection is a superior court of record and therefore functions alongside the mainstream court service, with the same powers, rights, privileges and authority as the High Court. It has a President at its head and a Vice President, Senior Judge and a central administration (Registry) based in London. Cases are heard by specially nominated High Court, Circuit and District Judges. The Court has hearing venues in a handful of locations in England and Wales so that hearings can be nearer to the people concerned.

Who can apply to the Court?

Generally, people will need to get the Court's permission before they make an application. People who do not need permission include the person who lacks capacity, the donor or attorney of an LPA and a Court-appointed deputy.

What declarations can the Court make?

The Court has wide-ranging powers – for example, it can:

- Make declarations as to whether or not a person has capacity to make a particular decision;
- Make orders affecting people who lack capacity;
- Appoint deputies to act and make decisions on behalf of people who lack capacity; and
- Remove deputies or attorneys acting under a LPA who act improperly.

Some issues will always go to the Court of Protection, even if no one objects to them. These will be where there are serious medical issues such as organ donation, sterilisation, abortion or possible death. The Court of Protection must see all such cases to check their legality.

Court-appointed deputies

The Court of Protection has the power to appoint an individual (the deputy) to make decisions on behalf of a person who lacks capacity in his or her best interests in certain circumstances – for example, where no valid LPA exists or there is a serious dispute among carers. A deputy could be a family member, carer or any other person who the Court finds suitable.

Deputies will be able to take decisions on financial, welfare and healthcare as authorised by the Court, but there are specific restrictions and limitations on their powers – for example:

1) The deputy will not be able to carry out an act that is intended to restrain the person concerned unless certain conditions are satisfied – which are similar to Section 6 in relation to acts in connection with care or treatment;

2) The deputy does not have power to make a decision on behalf of the person if he or she knows or has reason to believe that the person has capacity to make the decision or do the act in question;

3) The deputy cannot be given a power or make a decision inconsistent with a donee of an LPA;

4) The deputy cannot refuse consent to life-sustaining treatment.

The deputy remains accountable to the Court of Protection for his or her actions. The Court has power to discharge the order appointing a deputy at any time if it decides the appointment is no longer in the best interests of the person lacking capacity. The Public Guardian is responsible for the supervision of deputies and for supporting them in their role.

Court of Protection visitors

The Court can also send visitors to see people who have attorneys or deputies acting for them. The visitors can check on someone's general welfare or investigate suspected problems. They can offer support and advice, and report to the Court or the Office of the Public Guardian.

Office of the Public Guardian

The MCA established a new statutory office, the Public Guardian, who is appointed by the Lord Chancellor and has a range of functions contributing to the protection of persons who lack capacity. The Public Guardian is supported by the Office of the Public Guardian, which is an executive agency of the Ministry of Justice.[12]

The functions of the Public Guardian are set out in Section 58 of the Act and include:

- Establishing and maintaining a register of LPAs and Court of Protection orders appointing deputies;

- Supervising deputies appointed by the Court of Protection;

- Dealing with complaints about the way in which a donee or deputy is exercising his or her powers.

The Office of the Public Guardian provides a Customer Service Unit, which is the first point of contact and advice for anyone who needs information, help or guidance on the role or procedures of the Public Guardian or the Court of Protection.

The Public Guardian Board, which consists of a judge of the Court of Protection and lay members, is appointed by the Lord Chancellor to scrutinise and review the Public Guardian's work and make recommendations.

Ill treatment and neglect

The MCA introduced a new criminal offence of ill treatment or neglect of a person who lacks capacity. A person found guilty of such an offence may be liable to imprisonment for a term of up to five years.

Research involving people lacking capacity to consent

The MCA provides that research involving, or in relation to, a person lacking capacity may be lawfully carried out if an 'appropriate body' (normally a Research Ethics Committee) agrees that the research is safe, relates to the person's condition and cannot be done as effectively using people who have

---

[12]   See http://www.publicguardian.gov.uk

mental capacity. The research must produce a benefit to the person that outweighs any risk or burden. Alternatively, if it is to derive new scientific knowledge, it must be of minimal risk to the person and be carried out with minimal intrusion or interference with his or her rights.

Carers or nominated third parties must be consulted and agree that the person would want to join an approved research project. If the person shows any signs of resistance or indicates in any way that he or she does not wish to take part, the person must be withdrawn from the project immediately.

Decisions excluded from the MCA

Family relationship decisions

The MCA expressly does not govern any of the following matters:

- Consent to marriage or civil partnership;
- Consent to sexual relations;
- Consent to divorce or dissolution of marriage on the grounds of two years' separation;
- Consent to placing a child for adoption or making an adoption order;
- Discharging parental responsibilities in relation to matters not concerning the child's property; and
- Giving consent under the Human Fertilisation and Embryology Act 1990.

Voting

The MCA also does not allow decisions on voting, at an election or referendum, to be made on behalf of a person who lacks capacity to vote.

Unlawful killing or assisting suicide

Section 62 also states that nothing in the MCA is to be taken to affect the law relating to unlawful killing or assisting suicide. This means that therefore no one can ask for and be given unlawful procedures under the MCA, such as assistance in committing suicide.

Children and young people

Most of the MCA does not apply to children under 16 years of age. The care and treatment of children under 16 are generally covered by the common law. The two exceptions to this are:

- The Court of Protection powers to make decisions about property or finances on behalf of under 16s who lack capacity, where the child is likely to still lack capacity to make these decisions when he or she reaches 18; and

- The criminal offence of ill treatment and neglect applies to victims under 16.

Most of the MCA applies to young people aged 16-17 years old. The three exceptions are:

- Only people aged 18 and over can make LPAs;

- Only people aged 18 and over can make Advance Decisions to refuse treatment;

- The Court of Protection can make a statutory Will only for people aged 18 and over.

Mental Health Act 1983

The MCA cannot be used to give a person, who lacks capacity, treatment for a mental disorder or consent to such treatment on his or her behalf, if the person is detained and being treated under Part 4 of the Mental Health Act 1983. However, the MCA could still apply to patients detained under the Mental Health Act in other situations – for example, where someone who has been detained lacks capacity to make a decision, such as consenting to treatment for a physical condition, or making financial decisions.

The MCA Code of Practice

The legal framework provided in the MCA is supported by the Code of Practice, which provides guidance and information to all those working with and caring for adults who lack capacity, including family members, professionals and carers.

The Code has statutory force and the following categories of people have a legal duty to have regard to it when acting in relation to a person who lacks capacity:

1. The donee or attorney of a lasting power of attorney;

2. A deputy appointed by the Court of Protection;

3. Anyone carrying out research in accordance with the Act;

4. An Independent Mental Capacity Advocate;

5. Anyone working in a professional capacity – such as a doctor or social worker;

6. Anyone receiving payment for work – for example, a care assistant.

If these categories of people have not followed the relevant guidance in the Code then they are expected to give reasons why they have departed from it. Other people who are not placed under this legal duty will still be expected to follow the guidance in the Code – for example, informal carers or family carers.

Failure to comply with the Code can be used in evidence before a court or tribunal in any civil or legal proceedings, if relevant. This applies not only to those categories of people who have a duty to have regard to the Code but also to those who are not under such a duty.

Chapter 14

The Deprivation of Liberty Safeguards

The Mental Capacity Act 2005 was amended by the Mental Health Act 2007 to introduce a new legal framework for deprivations of liberty. This framework is known as 'The Deprivation of Liberty Safeguards' and it enables people who lack capacity to consent to the arrangements made for their care or treatment, to be deprived of their liberty in a care home or a hospital if it is considered necessary in their best interests.

A supplement to the *Mental Capacity Act 2005 Code of Practice*, which covers the deprivation of liberty safeguards, provides guidance and information about how the framework should operate in practice (the *DOL Code of Practice*).[1] As is the case for the main *Mental Capacity Act Code of Practice*, certain categories of people are required to have regard to the relevant guidance in the *DOL Code of Practice*, including anyone acting in a professional capacity.

Background

The Deprivation of Liberty Safeguards were introduced as a result of a legal case, known as the 'Bournewood case' or 'HL v UK'. This concerned an autistic man (known as 'HL') with a learning disability, who lacked the

---

[1] Available for download at: http://www.dh.gov.uk/en/Publicationsandstatistics/ Publications/PublicationsPolicyAndGuidance/DH_085476?IdcService=GET_ FILE&dID=167082&Rendition=Web

capacity to consent to, or to refuse, admission to hospital for treatment.

In July 1999, HL was admitted to Bournewood Hospital for assessment and treatment of a mental disorder. Since he did not object or resist to the admission, HL was not detained under the Mental Health Act 1983 but was admitted informally in his best interests, in accordance with the common law doctrine of necessity. This was common practice at the time.

HL remained in hospital for several weeks and was prevented from leaving and denied access to his carers.

HL's carers, who had objected to the admission, brought legal proceedings against the Hospital Managers on the grounds of unlawful detention. This went through the appeal courts to the House of Lords, and then to the European Court of Human Rights.

In 2004, the European Court of Human Rights reached the following conclusions:

1. HL had been deprived of his liberty when he had been admitted informally to hospital;

2. His informal admission had not been in accordance with 'a procedure prescribed by law' and was therefore in breach of Article 5(1) of the European Convention on Human Rights (ECHR); and

3. There had also been a breach of Article 5(4) of the ECHR because HL was not able to apply to a court quickly to see if his deprivation of liberty was lawful.

To prevent similar breaches of the ECHR, the deprivation of liberty safeguards were introduced for people such as HL, who lack decision-making capacity and who need to be deprived of their liberty in order to provide care and treatment, but who cannot be detained under the Mental Health Act 1983. The safeguards were implemented in April 2009.

Where can deprivations of liberty take place?

Although the Bournewood case was about a patient who was admitted to a psychiatric hospital, the judgment has wider implications that extend to people who lack capacity and need to be deprived of liberty but do not require hospital treatment. The safeguards therefore apply to all hospitals (including acute hospitals and psychiatric hospitals) and care homes. The safeguards also apply regardless of whether the care or treatment has been publicly or privately arranged.

The deprivation of liberty safeguards do not, however, apply to people living in their own homes or in supported living arrangements other than a care home. In these cases, it is only lawful to deprive a person of his or her liberty following an order by the Court of Protection.

What is deprivation of liberty?

The question of whether a person has been, or is likely to be, deprived of his or her liberty is not straightforward, as the judgments of numerous legal cases (including the Bournewood case) demonstrate.

The judgment in the Bournewood case made it clear that the starting point must be the concrete situation of the individual concerned and account must be taken of a whole range of criteria such as the type, duration, effects and manner of implementation of the measure(s) in question.

There is a distinction in law between:

- A 'Deprivation of Liberty', which is unlawful unless authorised; and

- A 'Restriction of Liberty', which is lawful if carried out in accordance with the Mental Capacity Act (see chapter 13).

However, this distinction is merely one of degree or intensity and not one of nature or substance.

Chapter 2 of the *DOL Code of Practice* provides practical guidance on, and examples from case law of, what constitutes a deprivation of liberty. It also provides practical steps that can be taken to reduce the risk of a deprivation of liberty becoming necessary.

Who can be deprived of his/her liberty?

The Deprivation of Liberty Safeguards apply in England and Wales to people aged 18 and over, who:

- Are suffering from a mental disorder;

- Lack capacity to consent to the arrangements made for their care or treatment; and

- Need to be given care and treatment in circumstances that amount to a deprivation of liberty in a hospital or a care home, where this care and treatment are necessary to protect them from harm and are in their best interests.[2]

Authorisations for deprivations of liberty

The Deprivation of Liberty Safeguards provide two mechanisms for depriving a person of his/her liberty: 'Standard Authorisations' and 'Urgent Authorisations'.

1. Standard Authorisations

In most cases, a Standard Authorisation must be obtained before a person can be deprived of his or her liberty.

The procedure
The procedure for obtaining this can be summarised as follows:

1. The relevant hospital or care home (known as 'the Managing Authority') must complete an application for a Standard Authorisation when it appears likely that, at some point during the next 28 days, someone will need to be deprived of his or her liberty in order to be provided with care or treatment.

2. The application must be sent to the appropriate 'Supervisory Body'. This will be:

- The commissioning primary care trust (for hospitals in England);

- The Welsh Ministers or local health board (for hospitals in Wales); or

- The local authority (for care homes in England and Wales).

---

[2] The term 'best interests' is a legal concept and is defined in Section 4 of the Mental Capacity Act 2005 (see chapter 13)..

3. The Supervisory Body must then appoint a minimum of two independent assessors (one of whom must be a doctor with experience in mental disorder) to assess whether the criteria for a deprivation of liberty are satisfied (see below).

4. If the assessments conclude that the person meets the criteria, then the Supervisory Body must issue a Standard Authorisation for a deprivation of liberty. This can last up to 12 months. The length of a Standard Authorisation is decided by the Best Interests Assessor (see below).

The criteria

A Standard Authorisation can be issued only if a series of six assessments indicates the need to do so. These must be completed within 21 days, starting from the date on which the Supervisory Body receives the request from the Managing Authority, or in Wales, 21 days starting from the date that the assessors were instructed by the Supervisory Body.

The six assessments are as follows:

1. The Age Assessment The Age Assessment must confirm that the person is aged 18 or over. It can be undertaken by anyone who is eligible to be a Best Interests Assessor (see below).

2. The Mental Health Assessment The Mental Health Assessment must establish whether the relevant person is suffering from a mental disorder within the meaning of the Mental Health Act 1983 but disregarding the exclusion for learning disability. This means any disorder or disability of the mind (including all learning disabilities) but not including dependence on alcohol or drugs.

This Assessment must be carried out by a doctor who is approved under Section 12 of the Mental Health Act 1983 or has at least three years' post-registration experience in the diagnosis and treatment of mental disorder. In England, the doctors must also have completed the standard training for Deprivation of Liberty Mental Health Assessors.

3. The Mental Capacity Assessment The Mental Capacity Assessment must establish whether the person lacks the relevant decision-making capacity. For a Standard Authorisation to be issued, the person must lack capacity to decide whether or not to be accommodated in the relevant hospital or care home for the purpose of being given the relevant care or treatment. An assessment must be made of the person's capacity to make this decision at the time it needs to be taken.

The Mental Capacity Assessment can be undertaken by anyone who is eligible to be Mental Health or Best Interests Assessor (see below).

4. The Best Interests Assessment The Best Interests Assessment must establish whether:

- A deprivation of liberty is occurring, or going to occur;

- It is in the best interests of the relevant person to be deprived of liberty;

- A deprivation of liberty is necessary to prevent harm to the relevant person; and

- It is a necessary and proportionate response to the likelihood of the person suffering harm and the seriousness of that harm, for the person to be deprived of liberty.

The Best Interests Assessor must be an Approved Mental Health Professional, a social worker, nurse, occupational therapist or psychologist, who the Supervisory Body is satisfied has the necessary skills and experience to carry out this role.

The Best Interests Assessor can be an employee of the Supervisory Body or Managing Authority but cannot be involved in the care or treatment of the person being assessed.

5. The Eligibility Assessment The purpose of the Eligibility Assessment is to ensure that the relevant person cannot be dealt with more appropriately under the Mental Health Act 1983. In order to satisfy this requirement, the Assessor must establish that:

- The person is not detained in hospital under the Mental Health Act 1983;

- The Authorisation does not conflict with an obligation placed on the person by leave of absence, Guardianship, Supervised Community Treatment or conditional discharge, such as a requirement to live somewhere else; and

- The person could not be more appropriately detained under the Mental Health Act 1983. A Standard Authorisation could not be given to deprive someone of his or her liberty in a hospital for the purpose of treatment for a mental disorder, in circumstances where the Mental Health Act 1983 could be used – for example, if the person objects to deprivation of liberty, or is likely to object, and he/she meets the critieria for detention under Section 2 or Section 3 of the Mental Health Act 1983.

The Eligibility Assessment must be carried out by a doctor who is approved under Section 12 of the Mental Health Act 1983 or by a Best Interests Assessor who is also an Approved Mental Health Professional.

6. The No Refusals Assessment The purpose of the No Refusals Assessment is to establish whether the Standard Authorisation would conflict with other decision-making authority for that person. The assessor must therefore ensure that the deprivation of liberty is not inconsistent with a valid Advance Decision or any decision made by the person's donee under a Lasting Power of Attorney or Deputy appointed by the Court of Protection (see chapter 10).

This Assessment can be undertaken by anyone who is eligible to be a Best Interests Assessor.

If each of the six assessments comes to the conclusion that the relevant person meets the qualifying requirement to which the assessment relates, then the Supervisory Authority must give a Standard Authorisation.

Considerations for Supervisory Bodies when appointing Assessors
There must be a minimum of two Assessors. The Mental Health Requirement and the Best Interests Requirement must be assessed by different people.

None of the Assessors should have a financial interest in the case of the person being assessed nor can they be a relative of the person being assessed.

The *DOL Code of Practice* also recommends that the Supervisory Body should seek to avoid appointing Assessors in any conflict of interests situations that might bring into question their objectivity. It also suggests that knowledge of the experience of working with the same service-user client group and people from the same cultural background as the person being assessed may be relevant considerations when appointing Assessors.[3]

---

[3] Ministry of Justice and Department of Health, Mental Capacity Act 2005 Deprivation of Liberty Safeguards (2008) paras: 4.13 to 4.14.

Conditions

The Best Interests Assessor may recommend conditions that should be attached to the Standard Authorisation. The Supervisory Body must then decide which conditions, if any, will apply and the Managing Authority must ensure they are complied with. For example, the conditions may specify who the relevant person should have contact with, when he or she can go out, which behaviours are prohibited and any other issues related to the deprivation of liberty. The *DOL Code of Practice* recommends that any conditions must relate directly to the Deprivation of Liberty and should aim to impose the minimum necessary restraints.[4]

Form of Authorisation

A Standard Authorisation must be in writing and must state the following:

- The name of the relevant person;

- The name of the relevant hospital or care home;

- The period during which the authorisation is to be in force;

- The purpose for which the Authorisation is given;

- Any conditions subject to which the Authorisation is given;

- The reason why each qualifying requirement is met.

2. Urgent Authorisations

If it is not possible to obtain a Standard Authorisation, and the Managing Authority believes it is necessary to deprive a person of his or her liberty in his/her best interests before the Standard Authorisation process can be completed, then an Urgent Authorisation can be completed.

Criteria

In order to issue an Urgent Authorisation, the Managing Authority must:

- Have made a request for a Standard Authorisation, or be required to make such a request; and

- Believe that the need for the relevant person to be deprived of

---

[4] Ministry of Justice and Department of Health, Mental Capacity Act 2005 Deprivation of Liberty Safeguards (2008) paras: 4.74 to 4.75.

liberty is so urgent that it is appropriate for the detention to begin before the request is disposed of, or before the request is made.

The *DOL Code of Practice* is clear that an Urgent Authorisation should not be used where there is no expectation that a Standard Authorisation would be needed and where an Urgent Authorisation is being used simply to legitimise a short-term deprivation of liberty. Similarly, an Urgent Authorisation should not be used, for example, in an accident and emergency department or a care home, where it is anticipated that in a short period of time the person will no longer be in that environment.[5]

Effect of an Urgent Authorisation

An Urgent Authorisation enables the Hospital or Care Home Managers to authorise themselves to deprive a person of liberty for up to seven days, pending the completion of the Standard Authorisation Assessment. The Supervising Body can extend this for a further seven days whilst the Standard Authorisation Assessments are carried out.

The Managing Authority decides the period for which the Urgent Authorisation is given but it must not exceed seven days. In exceptional cases this can be extended to a maximum of 14 days by the Supervisory Body.

Form of the Urgent Authorisation

An Urgent Authorisation must be in writing and must state the following things:

- The name of the relevant person;

- The name of the relevant hospital or care home;

- The period during which the Authorisation is to be in force;

- The purpose for which the Authorisation is given.

Representatives and Advocates

Once a Standard Authorisation has been given, the Supervisory Body must appoint a Representative for the person being deprived of liberty.

---

[5] Ministry of Justice and Department of Health, Mental Capacity Act 2005 Deprivation of Liberty Safeguards (2008) paras: 6.3 to 6.4.

Role of the Representative

The role of the Representative is to maintain contact with the person and to represent and support him or her in matters relating to the Standard Authorisation. The Representative has a right to require a review to be held, use the complaints procedure or appeal to the Court of Protection on the person's behalf.

Who can be a Representative?

A Representative can be chosen by:

- The person being deprived of his/her liberty, if he/she has capacity to make that choice;

- Their donee under a Lasting Power of Attorney or Deputy appointed by the Court of Protection, in cases where these powers are relevant; or

- The Best Interests Assessor or the Supervisory Body.

The Representative must be:

- 18 years old or over;

- Able to keep in contact with the relevant person; and

- Willing to be appointed.

The Representative cannot:

- Have a financial interest in the Managing Authority, or be a relative of someone who has a financial interest;

- Be employed by the care home where the relevant person is living, or be involved in providing services to the care home;

- Be employed by the hospital where the relevant person has been admitted and involved in his/her care and treatment; or

- Be employed by the Supervisory Body to work in a role related to the relevant person's care.

Where there is no Representative, the Supervisory Body must appoint an Independent Mental Capacity Advocate to undertake the function.

Role of the Independent Mental Capacity Advocate (IMCA)

Both the person who is deprived of liberty and his or her Representative have a right of access to an IMCA. The role of the IMCA is to help represent the relevant person and assist him/her, and his/her Representative, to understand the Authorisation and how to challenge it. The IMCA may also request that the Supervisory Body should review any of the qualifying criteria.

Duties to give information

Where a Standard Authorisation is given, the Supervisory Body must give a copy of the Authorisation to:

- The relevant person's Representative;
- The Managing Authority of the relevant hospital or care home;
- The relevant person;
- Any Section 39A IMCA;
- Every interested person consulted by the Best Interests Assessor.

Where a Standard Authorisation is not made following a request, the Supervisory Body must give notice to each of the following:

- The Managing Authority of the relevant hospital or care home;
- The relevant person;
- Any Section 39A IMCA;
- Every interested person consulted by the Best Interests Assessor.

Where a Standard Authorisation is given, the Managing Authority of the relevant hospital or care home must take such steps as are practicable to ensure that the relevant person understands all of the following:

- The effect of the Authorisation;
- The right to make an application to the Court of Protection;
- The right to request a review;
- The right to have an IMCA appointed;

- How to have an IMCA appointed.

Any written information given to the relevant person must also be given by the Managing Authority to the relevant person's Representative and where applicable his/her IMCA.

Where an Urgent Authorisation is given, the Managing Authority of the relevant hospital or care home must take such steps as are practicable to ensure that the relevant person understands all of the following:

- The effect of the Authorisation;
- The right to make an application to the Court of Protection.

Consent to treatment

While a Deprivation of Liberty Authorisation might be given for the purpose of providing treatment, the Deprivation of Liberty Authorisation does not authorise treatment. Any treatment given while the person is subject to a Deprivation of Liberty Authorisation, may be given only with the person's consent (if he or she has capacity to make this decision) or in accordance with a Best Interests Determination under the wider provisions of the Mental Capacity Act 2005 (see chapter 10).

Any treatment given while the person is subject to a Deprivation of Liberty Authorisation is not regulated by Parts 4 and 4A of the Mental Health Act 1983. The only exceptions to this are patients who are subject to Supervised Community Treatment and also under a Deprivation of Liberty Authorisation.

Reviews of the Deprivation of Liberty Authorisation

Who can request a review?

The Supervisory Body must carry out a review of a Standard Authorisation if a request is made by:

- The person deprived of liberty;

- His or her Representative; or
- The Managing Authority body – which is also under a duty to monitor the case of any person deprived of liberty, to see if the person's circumstances change. This may indicate the need for a review or discharge.

The Supervisory Body can also carry out a review at its own discretion.

Statutory grounds for review

The grounds for a review are that:

- The person no longer meets one of the six requirements for a deprivation of liberty set out above;
- As a result of a change in the person's circumstances it is appropriate to make changes to the conditions to which the Authorisation is subject; or
- The reasons why the person meets the qualifying requirements is different from the reasons given when the Standard Authorisation was given.

The review process

Once it receives a request for a review, the Supervisory Body must decide which of the qualifying requirements need(s) to be reviewed (if any) and arrange for a separate review assessment for each of these.

If the Supervisory Body decides that only the conditions attached to the Authorisation need to be changed and there is no need for a full reassessment of the best interests condition, it can vary the conditions as appropriate.

Assessors are allowed to rely upon existing assessments that are no more than a year old.

Outcome of the review

If any assessment determines that the conditions are not met, the Authorisation is terminated immediately. Once it ends, the Supervisory Body must inform:

- The relevant person;

- His or her Representative;

- The Managing Authority; and

- Any other relevant person named by the Best Interests Assessor.

A Deprivation of Liberty Authorisation can end before a formal review takes place. It can be ended immediately – for example, by changing the care regime. The Managing Authority would then apply to the Supervisory Body for a review and, if appropriate, formally terminate the Authorisation.

Rights of appeal

The Deprivation of Liberty Safeguards provide a right to appeal to the Court of Protection in certain circumstances.

1. Before an authorisation is given

The relevant person, his/her Representative or a donee of a Lasting Power of Attorney or Deputy appointed by the Court of Protection can apply (without permission) to the Court before an Authorisation has been issued asking it, for example, to determine whether the person has capacity or whether any act done or proposed to be done is lawful. Any other person must seek permission to take the case to Court.

2. After a Standard Authorisation has been given

The person, his/her Representative or a donee of a Lasting Power of Attorney or Deputy has the right to apply to the Court to determine:

- Whether the person meets one or more of the qualifying requirements;

- The length that the order is to be in force;

- The purpose for which the Standard Authorisation is given; or

- The conditions that are attached to the order.

Any other person must seek permission to take the case to Court.

The Court has the power to vary or terminate the Standard Authorisation, or direct the Supervisory Body to vary or terminate the Standard Authorisation.

3. After an urgent authorisation has been given

The person, his/her Representative or a donee of a Lasting Power of Attorney or Deputy has the right to apply to the Court of Protection to determine:

- Whether the Authorisation should have been given;

- The length that the order is to be in force; or

- The purpose for which the Standard Authorisation has been given.

The Court has the power to vary or terminate the Urgent Authorisation, or direct the Managing Authority to vary or terminate the Urgent Authorisation.

Unauthorised deprivations of liberty

If a person believes that he or she is being deprived of his/her liberty without an Authorisation being issued, or a third party believes that this has occurred, then he/she can write to the Managing Authority (using a standard letter), who must respond within 24 hours.

The person can also approach the Supervisory Body in cases where he/she has raised the matter with the Managing Authority and no application for a Deprivation of Liberty Authorisation has been made within a reasonable period. In such cases (unless there are good reasons not to do so), the Supervisory Body must arrange for a Best Interests Assessor to decide whether the person is deprived of liberty. This must be completed within seven days.

If the Best Interests Assessor concludes an unauthorised deprivation of liberty is taking place, then the full assessment must be completed as for any other Standard Authorisation.

If a person raises concerns about an unauthorised deprivation of liberty with the Supervisory Body, then the Supervisory Body must arrange an initial assessment and then, if necessary, ask the Managing Authority to apply for a Standard Authorisation.

Section 117 aftercare

The categories of people eligible to receive aftercare services under Section 117 of the Mental Health Act 1983 do not include people who are (or have been) subject to the Deprivation of Liberty Safeguards. However, a person who is entitled to Section 117 services would not lose that entitlement on the basis that a Standard or Urgent Authorisation had been issued.

Overlap with the Mental Health Act 1983

There is some overlap between the Deprivation of Liberty Safeguards and the powers under the Mental Health Act 1983. Although the Deprivation of Liberty Safeguards cannot apply to people who are detained in hospital under the Mental Health Act 1983, they may apply where a person is subject to the various community orders under the 1983 Act.

Where a person is on leave of absence or subject to Supervised Community Treatment, Guardianship or conditional discharge, an Authorisation for deprivation of liberty can be given as long as this is not inconsistent with an obligation placed on the person under the Mental Health Act 1983 – for example, a requirement to live somewhere particular.

Where the Authorisation relates to a deprivation of liberty in a hospital for the purpose of treatment for a mental disorder, then the person cannot be made subject to the Deprivation of Liberty Safeguards if he or she:

- Objects to being admitted to hospital and meets the criteria for detention under the Mental Health Act 1983. In such cases, the *DOL Code of Practice* suggests that it may be necessary to arrange an assessment to see if the person needs to be detained under the Mental Health Act.[6]

- Is on leave of absence or subject to Supervised Community Treatment or conditional discharge, where instead the powers of recall under the Mental Health Act can be used.

---

[6] Ministry of Justice and Department of Health, Mental Capacity Act 2005 Deprivation of Liberty Safeguards (2008) para: 4.56.

Index